MW01230770

Able Publishing

You can follow Dan at:
twitter.com/thatdankent

@thatdankent

to Barbara

thank you for
inspiring so much
poetry

and sorry
I wrecked
your car

1

some are
skywriters
others are simply
blowing smoke

page 6

2

epiphany
scars

page 62

3

a drowning at a
baptism

page 116

4

**smooth jazz
for martyrs**

page 164

5

**snow-boarding
over bell-curves**

page 210

6

**if you're gonna learn
to fly you'd better
learn to land**

page 256

some are skywriters
others are simply
blowing smoke

andante

every atom in me
thumps
as each electron
spins and strums
its neighbors like
a harp
in a world that wants
to tear
me
apart
I step out
into the dawn
held together like
a song

the fundamentals of skywriting

so you want to be
a skywriter?
you want to soar
above it all?

that's fine, son.

to soar so fully free,
to send a message
to so great a crowd,
so far and small
beneath your feet,
yet to remain
out of their reach,
while luring each
to look up to see
whatever message your
audacious heart wants
them to see?

that's all fine, son.

but, goddammit kid,
you've just gotta
spell the words right,
and you goddamn better
have something to say
worth looking up for.

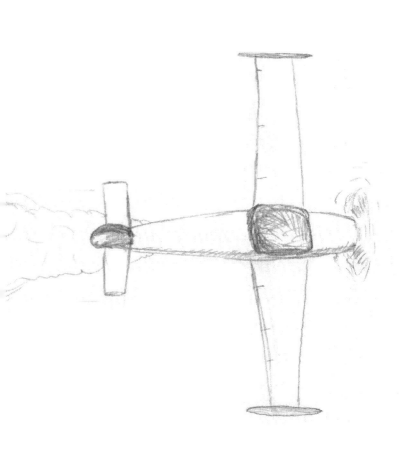

the balloon is too heavy for the helium

the party
is over.
I'll never write a good poem again.
there's no sense turning the page—
look at this garbage.
I bore myself to tears.
the audience is checking their watches
and fingering pixels on their phones.
if they could, they'd curse.

I should be glad with what I have.
my hand has birthed some decent verse—
a couple real gems even.
my pen once tap-danced across the page,
and the Holy Spirit would push
dazzling pictures through the ink.

I barely had to try!
I barely had to think!

but now those good old poems
mock me from the shelf.
I sit with grunts and strains,
like a constipated drunk,
and all that trickles out
are these black bile stains
and a sad lamenting pout
of an old man who's shrunk
to envying his younger self.

the lithp

I th'poke with a lith'p
when I th'tarted th'cool.

the th'pethialitht ath'ked mom:

"How could you not
do anything about
thith?"

Mom thaid: "It'th THO cute,
that'th why."

October flight lessons

it was sunnier and warmer
than normal.
Boxelder Bugs
covered everything
that faced the sun.

　"They're everywhere!"

in my ear,
in my hair,
in the pocket of my shirt.
one was even tryna' steal
a swig of my coffee.

we moved our chairs
to get away.
it didn't work.
they followed close behind.

one was flying toward my face.
I leaned to the left.
she shifted her path.
I leaned to the right.
I heard her tiny scream:

　"How do I fly this thing!"

a moment before
crashing into my cheek.

"The only time an aircraft has too much fuel on board is when it is on fire."

Charles Kingford Smith,
first man to make trans-Pacific flight from Australia to the US.
Charles divorced Thelma Eileen Hope in 1929, married Mary Powell in 1930, then disappeared somewhere over the Andaman Sea in 1935

imposters

the waitress brings
the coffee drink
sets it on the table
between my iphone and
my manuscript—
stacked there two-hundred
pages high.

I'm on my way
to deliver my book
to my friend Greg—
he's writing the Forward.

anyway, I'm sipping
my latte, enjoying
the tender hazelnut
flavor, when some Frank
Sinatra wannabe
on the cafe speakers
bellows out some buttermilk
verse.

it sounds lousy
to tell you the truth,
nothing like
Frank Sinatra
that's for sure.

anyway, Greg
has a great mind

and I admit
I have some awe,
and I'm sitting here
wondering,
you know,
if the book,
or if I,
are worthy of his
endorsement.

the waitress comes back,
brings my check,
takes my cup.
we talk about the music
and I mention
"it sorta sounds
like Frank Sinatra"

she looks down at me
as I gather up
my manuscript,
iPhone,
wallet,
keys,
and she informs me
the music playing
actually is Sinatra

"from his early days."

summer said it was just going to the store

sipping coffee
swallowing back
vague anger
that summer
abandoned me
to this gray flop
of a season

I know I know
look on the bright side
find what's good

but I did that
five months ago
it got all hot
bright and green
and then it winked
ruffled my hair
grabbed its keys
and disappeared

now I stand
in terror-stare
at winter's feet

designer journals

I was smiling off the fragments
of a lingering joke
as I dashed between the shelves
of *Barnes & Noble Books.*

something caught my eye.
I slammed the brakes,
stood up straight,
stepped back for a closer look
at a wall full of shelves
which held
preposterous journal
books.

a little sign said:
DESIGNER JOURNALS
and indeed they were.
so ornate,
so rustic,
so gaudy,
so nostalgic,
glitter on maps
and other opulence,
engraved on soft covers
with metal clasps
and fancy straps.

the smell of leather like
garlic bulbs inside

of sweaty socks.
each book resting firm
upon a wooden shelf,
like God's own diary
of himself.

I stood there churning my
perplexion,
wondering who
these people are
who actually think
they have thoughts
and things to say
about themselves
that might be worth
such brazen
ostentation.

the whole thing bothered me—
I scowled and had to write it down.
so I grabbed my coffee-stained
bent and battered pad
from out my tattered bag
and wrote this all right there
on the carpet kneeling
in that spot.

thanks for reading!

HOW TO GET PEOPLE TO LIKE YOU

we get so confused.
we walk in a fog.
we get so alone.
don't know what to do.
folks ask me all the time:

> *How do I get people*
> *to like me?*

the first step,
of course:
convince total strangers
to engage you,
to talk to you,
to want your attention.

and this is dumb-simple to do
once you know simple truths.
just walk around town,
or the mall,
or the grocery store,
with headphones on,
lost in the nourishing light
of a podcast,
or enchanted in the euphoric spell
of some nocturne.

I guarantee,
the moment they see

you're flamboyantly free,
in your own world,
dozens will appear
from the sides and the rear,
from behind discount racks,
from out of the mirror,
and will suddenly have
oodles of things
to tell you about.

they'll tug on your sleeve,
they'll gyrate their jaws,
they'll throw out a hand
to get you to pause.
as soon as they see
you're content just to be
in your own zone,
they'll elbow and shove
to wedge themselves in it
and shrink at your feet
soft and unhidden.

human brains evolved
then man created the wheel
it's been downhill since

the chase

chase your dreams, chase
your dreams,
everybody telling everybody:

CHASE YOUR DREAMS,

with passion and vigor,
with hearts
racing.

don't give up
on your dreams,
they say,
to whomever they
are facing.

yet everywhere I look,
nobody tells anybody how
to find a dream
worth chasing.

MY DAY

I wouldn't say the bar was packed,
but it was lively enough.
I had a bottle of beer—
more a prop than anything,
I'm not much of a drinker.
I was waiting for the band
to start their set,
DOUG OTTO & THE GETAWAYS.
I knew the drummer.

anyway, this Somali guy
was out on the dance floor
doing the craziest thing.
I took a swig of beer and
watched him
meander the crowd
handing out
what appeared to be
money bills.

sure enough he came to me,
holding out a five dollar bill.
I shook my head and
waved my hand,
but he insisted the gift
and said with zealous force
and melody:

"TODAY IS YOUR DAY,
TOMORROW WILL BE MINE"

I acquiesced,
to be polite,
and he was pleased,
and disappeared
into the crowd.

I fondled the bill
in my fingers
to ensure it was real,
or to see if it was marred
with marketing prompts,
but, none of that at all.
the bill was clean.

I swigged my beer and tried
to spot the man again,
but he was gone.

so I just sat speculating,
contemplating a cause—
why one needs
to explain these things
I don't know
but that's how it goes.

*he's obviously manic,
or maybe he's stoned,*

I thought with a nod,

or mentally ill
in some other way.

the bar grew loud
when the band came out.
I finished my beer,
got up from my stool,
went to the urinal
and stood there
facing the concrete blocks,
pissing and smirking until
I uncovered a silly resent—
one I'm ashamed to admit.

I've worked hard
my whole life,
and five dollars
is a crap-lousy payoff
for my supposed day.

Seasonal Paranoia Disorder

eyes askance
I flinch and twitch
this time of year
creeps me out

spiders
 spiders
  spiders

they stand a fraction of my size
yet I'm no match for them
with their empty hearts
and all their wicked eyes

spiders
 spiders
  spiders

creeping out the back
of a long hot summer
of gluttonous feasting
on the bones of endless bugs
with winter coming fast
now too fat for their ghastly nets
vile vagabonds
angry guilty desperate
all on the move
out the corner of
each of my
nervous eyes

the dirt pile

people love our pile of dirt
a mighty truck dumped the pile
near the foot of our drive
folks gawk as they go by
and sometimes stop to talk

they want to know our plans
for it
they want to know what's in it
they want to know its character
they want to know its purpose
they want some for themselves
maybe just a scoop or two?

they tell me of their compost heaps
they tell me all their garden plans
they see our pile
their eyes go wide
they rub their hands
they smile

and when they're gone I grasp the shovel
jab the pile
lift a heap
into the barrow

jab, lift, dump
jab, lift, dump
jab, lift, dump

grateful for a God
who also loved a pile of dirt
and kissed it with a special breath

a God who longs to know
its character and
all about
its plans

a writing day prayer

this planet Earth
of yours oh Lord
a big roundish
battle zone

it orbits the sun
but rotates around
a dollar sign

greed and ambition
have infected
every mind
destroyed forests
tainted oceans
wasted time

I know we don't have
a whole lot longer
before you come back
to collect
to correct
to condemn
I know such vile
wicked greed
will not stand

but I ask oh Lord
please hold back
stand down
for a short while more

until I get this book
for which I have toiled
completed and
published

hey listen!
you're in it!
you are the star!

it's all about you
and your goodness
and your love and—
well I really think
it's going to sell
like crazy

I read these poets

who light their nights on fire
with outrageous desire
liquor
lovers
laughter
testing all extremes
feeling every thing to feel
wasting every thing to waste
and reaching every high they chase

they don't mean that much to me
I'm not impressed
I'm not inspired
I don't connect

I guess I'm even keel—
oh sure I've got a thing
for cookies freshly baked
and crave my morning coffee
I've even cuddled-up
and gotten kissy
with some sexy babes
but nothing like
these
poetic passion-slaves

I read these poets
kicking their shambles around
searching for clues to solve

the puzzles of their hearts
unlocking shallow mysteries
trying to find the causes
of their chaoses
their uproarious nights
their laborious days
their radioactive emotions—
turbulent troubles I just don't get

oh sure I've been a moral fool
but it's not so puzzling to me
sin just feels so very good
(and oh how lazy I can be!)
I give in then have regret
for whatever damage I have done
but do my best and I repent
and always get back up again

I read these poets each
who take themselves
so seriously
the fanatic romantic
the mirror captive
the neglected child
attention seekers
trouble makers fashionably wild
suicide fakers
who write their prose
with tears and blood
squeezed from their moods
humorless dopes who try

to rub their sadness onto you
who get charged up
if readers cry

I read these masters of
poetic verse
who decorate so many pages
with all the colors of their woe
I read them across
a yawning divide

I'm a fairly happy guy
the darkness prowls *out there*
we just have to keep it
from getting inside

I read these poets who
parade their broken lives
which bring them great acclaim
awards
fellowships
fame

I read their eloquent laments
of their many bondages
but feel myself mostly free

I read these poets but perhaps
they should be reading me

the enemy is too small to see

look at this guy:
"Welcome to Holiday," he says,
showing me his greasy face
and lazy eyes.

would you suck this guy's fingers?
or lick his palms?

I adjust my products in my hands.
I have 2 cans of soda
and a bottle of water,
and I hold them out,
barcodes exposed,
hoping he shoots them
with his scanner gun,
hoping he doesn't try
to get all ambitious
and grab each one
with his pale moist hands
to hold under the barcode light.

it's just that, I find,
they always want to grab
the top of the can,
or the mouth of the bottle
(right where my lips will soon land),
and who knows where
this dude's hand
has just been?

maybe it caught a ferocious sneeze.
maybe one of its fingers
shook like crazy in his hairy ear
to mollify an intense
wax-secretion-itch.
or maybe he wiped his ass with too little
tissue—who knows?

all I know is I wouldn't lick his palms
or suck his chubby fingers.
so why would I want him to touch
my bottles or cans?

I'm holding them out.
he reaches for a can.
I pull back a tad.
he huffs frustration through his nose,
grabs his pricing blaster,
shoots each item,
asks me if I want a bag.

I don't.

I just give him the cash
and I dash
out the door
across the parking lot,
get in my car where I
look close at the lip
of my can for smudges,

or other anomalies—
a coward to unseen foes,
and mindful of fears
I've yet to outgrow.

doors doors doors

I'm done with doors
in public
I'm not opening doors
anymore
not for people I don't know

it's just more trouble
than it's worth

say you go and open a door
for some sweet gal
I guarantee
a trainload of tourists
will appear
from nowhere
and you'll get stuck there
frittering your day
as the sun goes down
and one tourist after another
nods their appreciation
as they enter the place
cameras close to their
face

and you know what's worse?
when they open the door
for you
say you get out of your car
after parking
they see you coming

through their binoculars
and with their big holy grin
they stand their holding
that silly door
just standing there
grinning and
watching and
waiting and
grinning and
watching and
waiting
as you make your way
compelled to quicken
your private pace
as they goad you on
with their holy face
and friendly nods
as Jesus and his holy saints
smile down
from tender clouds
at this modern-day
martyr

no
I'm done with doors

especially for women
with their purses and hats
and their complicated catch-22s
who see you near the door

and either assume
you will
(and if you don't
then you
good sir
are certainly no
gentleman)
or they assume you won't
(and if you do
then they assume
you must be some remnant of
a sad old patriarchy
just some narrow-minded dope
animated by old
oppressions)

take this note down
if I am coming in
or if I am going out
put my mind at ease
and leave me the hell
alone

I'm done with doors
so everyone please
just open
your own

the orb

I have this orb of hurt
about the size of a plum
that throbs somewhere deep
in the rear of my psyche

the saddest things trigger it
like today
it was a turtle on the road
driven over many times

a gentle traveler
whose armor
whose defense
whose home
was simply not enough
to guard against
all of us who roam
upon our hell-bent drunken journeys
of self-discovery
of self-fulfillment
of self-development
of self-actualization

a gentle traveler
who only wanted to get
back to the marsh pond
for her daily swim
who had no boasts
or ambitions
or American Dreams

or retirement plans
who was rather content
just as she was
who now lay there crushed
flattened by the evil
that is done under the sun
by heartless machines
of much larger spirits
far less mature

YOU WANT TO SOAR...

...ABOVE IT ALL?

counter weight

Felicia,
at the cash register,
smacked bubble-gum,
boasted big
flamboyant hair,
and girth that rubbed over
the top of the counter.

I was third in line—
bottled water and
Peanut M&Ms
in my hand.

Felicia looked down
with bored eyes
at some customer-lady
digging deep into the labrynth
of her shiny red purse,
until she looked up
and directed a mumble
right at Felicia.

Felicia just said,
"Mmm-hmmm,"
then turned away.

The line grew
behind me out
to the Hershey bars.
Felicia reached up,

stretching high,
squeezed a red pack
of cigarettes,
and turned back
as the line
had now grown
to the licorice ropes.

Then customer-lady mumbles
something else.
"Mmm-hmmm,"
Felicia says,
and turns as the line
is now behind
the pretzel station.

Felicia steps toward
the lottery case,
and the line
has now gone out
the door and past
the fuel pumps.

Felicia takes another
step as a family
joins the growing row
of customers.

The streetlights
flicker on.

Felicia takes another step.

The line is now down
past the Taco Bell
as Felicia tears a ticket
for lottery prizes,
and turns back
to face the register.

The patrons shift
their bodyweight
back-and-forth
all up and down
the chain like EKG
energy, and the line
has now protruded
into downtown
Saint Paul.

Our earth rotates
at a ferocious pace—
about a thousand and
forty miles per hour—
Felicia moves
step-by-step,
from scratch-offs
to tobacco boxes,
and takes the cash,
and gives change back,
at just about

one-one-thousandth
miles per hour—
to counteract
cosmic forces
and keep the earth
and universe
from unraveling
into total chaos.

nothing good happens after 8 or so

all the parties
have disappeared—
I don't know where they went

I thought they were a celebration
of life
of friends
something to do
a sacred event
for the vital among us

but all this time
I come to find
parties are another

lie

insincere gatherings
I guess
for mating—
breeding cages
as it were
and now
that all of them have found
their blessed match
their splendid mate
they've no need
for parties
anymore

and as for partners
I've found mine
5 years now
along the line
we have been wed

the sun's gone down
it's almost nine
we may as well
go to bed

this poem is like others I have written

we stopped at this Starbucks
in Tomah Wisconsin
right over there next to the Dollar Tree
and the Champion Auto Parts
Shelby took my order
and I thought:
I swear I know her

but no

that was someone 30 years ago
in fact her coworkers too
I recognized each one
and the dozen or so customers

that guy
this kid
and both those gossiping women

franchise folks
I guess
in a franchise world
each one a clone
of someone before

B sips her latte
I sip on mine
she and I
obviously each
one-of-a-kind

earning cookies

I'm swishing through
this grocery store,
wishing I'd written more,
or written really anything even,
but
W R I T E R'S B L O C K.

I make my way
toward the glow
of a bakery display
to get a cookie
I don't deserve
(having written nothing).

I walk fast
(I always have—
especially when
cookies are in play)
and I pass
between displays
of baguettes and bread,
when a little girl
pushing behind a kid-size cart,
running right at me,
brings her buggy
to a chaotic stop,
an inch or so
before my knee.

I stop to assess
the incident
and am about to say
"such an impressive
driver you are."

but before those words
could come out
(they're up my throat
and scratching
the backs
of my teeth)
her mother leaps over
to scold her.

"YOU'D BETTER WATCH
WHERE YOU'RE GOING
YOUNG LADY!"

mom then prostrates
herself before me
with oozing and foaming
apology,
but I just slink away.

see here's the thing:
her little girl really was watching
where she was going—
she stopped in time!

whatever though,

what can you do?

now I'm standing
face-to-face
with the bakery case,
which boasts
pastries and sweets,
and I'm thinking
how hard life must be
if we must feel guilt
not just for wrongs,
but also for
their possibility.

I pull a wax tissue
from the box,
extract a cookie
from the case
(the sassy one
with M&Ms),
then place it in my cart
and grin
like a kid,
convinced now,
because of this
poem right here,
and with regards
to the cookie:

I've earned this.

good lines

imagine me dragging leaves
with a rake over my frozen lawn
or pushing a shopping cart
through the grocery store parking lot
when some clever phrase
slaps me on the forehead
or a moving thought
warms my heart
or maybe a certain play of words
dances in my mouth as I
whisper them out

  I gotta write that down
  I say
  I could use that somewhere
  I tell myself

well now I'm running out
of paper scraps
cursed
with a burden
of more good lines than I can use

scraps of paper and
fragmented thoughts
blow around my desk
fill my notebook pages
or fall from my pockets
when I pull out my keys

you might call it poetic abuse
so many good lines
lines I'll never use
lines that gather dust
and grow double chins
lines that lose their spark
lines that get dumb and thin

but I keep them
these hoarded lines
I don't know why

someday my wife will find them
long after I die
she'll find them laying all around
when she's moving books
or redecorating a room
and she'll pick one up
read it with raised brow
then scratch her head
before throwing it out

I have too many lines
and I know these lines
will come to nothing in the end

yes I know things I don't want to know
I have too many lines and
I may as well
let them go

new iPad

B fell asleep on the couch
I'm sitting Indian style
upstairs on our bed
typing all this on my new iPad

every new writing device
changes a writer
I don't doubt it
did Twain ever switch to a typer?
did Whitman ever type?
I know Hemingway did
then reached for the gun
and Bukowski bought a computer
then died shortly after

it's not autumn yet
so I keep the window open
the neighbor across the street
inhaled too much of whatever he's smoking
and now coughs like a tractor
that just won't start

I remember standing in the store
facing all the new illuminated screens
fantasizing about writing on this iPad
just staring at its lines and curves
wondering what marvelous things
I could write

so far
only this

"I have seen the science I worshiped, and the aircraft I loved, destroying the civilization I expected them to serve."

Charles Lindbergh,
American aviator, military officer, author, inventor, and activist. Made first non-stop flight from New York to Paris

we exist forever in the middle of a three act play

the world
was once
enchanted
  the people
  dedicated

but now
the world
is slanted
  the people
  medicated

don't take
your life
for granted
  the people
  will soon
  be liberated

first flight of a monarch

when her wings dry
and she takes that long
awaited flight

—having freed herself from
that chrysalis
prison—

she must think
all those many many days
of crawling
nothing but
a dream.

epiphany scars

the telescope

I was an astronomer
for a short time,
somewhere around
age nine I'd say.
you'd walk into the room,
or pass me at the laundromat,
and I'd tell you all about
the rings of Saturn
or about that famous birthmark
on Jupiter.

later that year
for Christmas
Mom bought me a telescope
and I was so excited
I cried.
or maybe I didn't,
I don't remember. But,
I know I'd run to the window
again-and-again
to see if darkness yet
had crept across the sky.

when finally the sky
hung black, with specks of light,
I set the scope
up on its legs
out front by the steps
pointed it up
toward Mars.

what did I expect to see,
as I leaned my head
to the lens?

Yes, I admit,
my hopes were grandiose.

I imagined this scope
something like an eye-rifle,
if that makes sense,
that would shoot my mind out to the lights,
to the moon and beyond,
above the hard dome
of the known.

I must've thought I'd see
new worlds with
new peoples in new cities,
or some other marvel
to fascinate.

I really thought the scope would show
me something great,
or magical,
but all it really did,
no matter how I turned
the focus knobs,
was make that speck
of glowing rice inflate

to a fuzzy reddish-white
bb pellet.

then it was bed time.
I set the scope aside,
planning to come back
to try again soon,
but never did—
you know how it goes,
it sat unused
in the corner
of the room,
full of promise, but
lacking the zoom
to facilitate
my great escape.

the travel agent said there'd be a buffet

I'm on a boat
full of actors
with life jackets
paddle-oars
sunglasses

The USS LOL

breaching the shores
of what looks like hell

my shift at work was cancelled and I went for a walk

out come the puffy coats
folks look like chubby cherubs
and leaves on trees
turn outrageous shades—
electric lemon
neon brick—
and squirrels get
desperate
  and so do I
    and so do I

but I'm old enough to know
after the snow
warmth will return
and all the anorexic trees
will get obese and green
and butterflies will flutter by
(like levitating bow-ties)
and crowds of crows will dawdle
on long black power lines
like surplus periods and commas
as I keep walking by
passing thru the changes
riding a rhythm of heartbeats
through the best parts of God's
award-winning
creation

**I am uncomfortable with inaction,
she is uncomfortable with risk**

it's a smudge
on the glass
between us
and we try
but
can't decide
if it's on
her side
or mine.

TO SOAR SO FULLY FREE...

oar sores

look at us
rush hour traffic
our daily wait
our daily tax
our daily fritter

to a bird we look
like a river of boulders
to God
a river of shame

I release the brake
I depress the brake
release the brake
tap the gas
depress the brake
like everyone else
on this asphalt river—
modern day galley hands
row-row-rowing our boats
to our promised lands

Bvv Bvvvvv

it was another day
White Bear Avenue
by Maplewood Mall
the stoplight was red
  Bvvv Bvv Bvvvvvv

an odd car before me
rumbled melodic bass
while sections of that car
moved up and down
hydraulically
mechanically
involuntarily
with the deep wide rhythm
  Bvv Bvvvvvvvvv

other drivers
could feel the bass
and so could I
I could feel it on my earlobes
I could feel it on my crotch
I could feel it on my spine
  Bvv Bvvvvvv Bvv

the lady in the Escalade
rolled her windows up
some dude in an Audi
looked the other way
the Volvo woman
turned up her tinny tunes

as that awkward clunker
kept coughing out the bass
  Bvvvvvvvv Bvv Bvvvvvvvvv

like a warning siren
like prophetic morse code
like some modern day John
the Baptist
offering the repentant a baptism
of bass
  Bvv Bvvvvvvvv

the messenger idled there
in his anointed lowrider
shaking all beneficiaries
of this country's systems of oppression
agitating the power franchises
of coddled capitalists
drilling an urgent message
deep into our bones:

  YOUR TIME IS ALMOST UP

  Bvvv Bvvv Bvvv

the light turned green
I followed close behind
as he rumbled through our town
I clicked my radio off
and rolled my windows
down

"There are times when you devote yourself to a higher cause than personal safety."

John Glenn, *aviator, engineer, astronaut, and the first American to circle Earth in space. In 1989 a stranger punched Glenn in the face on television. The stranger did this to raise awareness of various prophetic dreams he was experiencing. The dreams involved earthquakes and the Pope.*

let's not get ahead of ourselves

some days
I doubt
eternality,

infinite
tomorrows,

days-upon-days
everlasting.

oh of course
GOD is wholly
everlasting
(I'm not dumb).

he's up there
stoned
on immortality.

and I get
his desire for
companionship,
I mean just to pass
the time,
but with us?
forever?
I have doubts.

I just left
this woodsy coffee shop

where a guy went on and on
and on and on
about stocks,
passive income,
getting rich.

another guy
seemed really pissed.
for what?
who knows?
but then this guy
wanted me to be
pissed off too,
but I wasn't —
so his anger grew.

some days I doubt
eternality,
endless starts
without stops.

it's just that
most people
get real dull
at about ten
minutes,

forty-five minutes
tops.

I wear plain black t-shirts

saw this guy
couple days ago—
total moron.
and I'm not being mean.
I have proof.
He wore a shirt
with one word
across the chest:

    G E N I U S.

as any genius
will tell you:
putting GENIUS
on your shirt
raises expectations,
prompting everyone
to come to you
with ev'ry silly little thing,
ev'ry problem they need
someone else to solve.

any genius knows,
if you really must
put a word across
your shirt or chest,
be careful with the word you pick—
in fact, make the word:

    I D I O T.

ATTENTION VISITORS:

if I'm not around when you get here,
make yourself at home.
sorry for the mess.
and when you wander
into my writing room,
I'm sure you'll think:

Wow, this guy's a slob.

but I'm really not.
I'm tidy, orderly—
sterile as underwear, new in the box!
it's just that I've been working
on this big dumb book
for half a decade.
notecards blow around
like autumn leaves,
stacks of massive books
stand like random roman pillars
here and there,
hoodies and flannels
hang from racks and hooks,
charts and pages taped
to walls and whiteboards
like crime investigations,
crumpled balls of paper
scattered toward a basket
(I shoot about eighty percent),
a dumbbell sits beside a wall
(its partner sits downstairs),

a hundred pens and markers
lay waiting for their chance
to dance across my pages,
a vacuum attachment rests
on the floor by the vent with a note:

FIX ME PLEASE   :)

it's been there since spring.
but once this book is done,
all these fragments
will find a home,
these books will be returned.
I'll wipe down the desk,
vacuum up the dusty floor,
replace the bulb,
fix the door.

you should come back then,
when I've hidden away
all my personal effects.
I'm sure you'll think:

Wow, this guy's got it all together.

yes, please come back then—
the day after this book
is finally done,
and before I've started
on my next.

writing can be hard
especially transitions
raccoons eat crickets

The Royal 10

when I was six
or maybe seven
I first typed
on grandpa's
antique Royal 10

indestructible
black cast iron
with gloss letters
on white circles
held up to me
on dainty levers

an arm swings
at custom speed
toward the page
in total synch
with pressing down
a given key

if you're shy
or too passive
the letters fail
to press the ink
onto the page
—and a change of mind's
a total pain

when you'd write
you had to be sure

of your thoughts
you'd just have to be
convicted

you had to say what you mean
mean what you say

the dark machine
beckoned me
I hit some keys
began to write
by compulsion
a kind of fever

catapulted thoughts
through fancy dancing
mechanical things
like spider legs
weaving webs

I couldn't spell
worth a damn
or organize
my wild thoughts
but typed on
and on and on
(I couldn't stop)

pattering words
on fettered paper

like icy rain
like punching
smug and haughty faces

those were still the Reagan years
and we were all neck deep
in Cold War fever dreams
mere moments before
Microsoft Word and the printer
infiltrated planet earth
to extirpate
the mechanical fire
of the Royal 10

I loved that thing
I loved how I could watch
each idea coalesce
from fractured pieces
tossed forward from the tips
of steel swords
to unify
on virgin paper

but now the words
materialize
upon a screen
without ink
without gears
without swords
without reason

now I stare at ev'ry word and line
and I've no clue
just how they're made
or from where they came
or even if they're mine

Serendipitous Exiles

the world had gone to shit
warfare starvation violence
families hustling for a crumb
little girls sold for sex
little boys with heavy guns
entire towns on shaky boats
fleeing bombs leaving homes
entire tribes without schools
who'll never learn to read
bibles fables poetry
and all our leaders drunk
on possibilites
of war and war
technologies

I'm grateful I was born
where I was born:
Minnesota
in the middle of North America
shrouded by mild
miles of plenty
in every direction you can look

and here I am hiking
a journey born of leisure
a journey born of wonder
a journey born of whimsy
through Lake Elmo Reserve
protected from the cold
by layers of special clothes

the grass is frosted
I can see my breath

then there behind a tree
I see a standing deer
a 4-point buck
from there to here
about 10 feet or so
deer hunting season
in full swing
macho tough guys
shooting out their minds
in silly camouflage
but here in the reserve
hunting's not allowed
and the buck watches
every move I make
measuring my pace
with a look upon his face
like the look upon my own
grateful yet guilty
for our safe place
in our dangerous world
our lucky little homes
we never even chose

turns out the people we see on the news are real

remember in the nineties on the news
when that American kid got busted in Singapore
for vandalism and they caned him
and Americans were outraged?

I met that kid a few months later
(right after his infamous punishment).
I was a busboy at this hotshot restaurant
sitting in the break room when he appeared.

He says to me, "I'm Michael Fay. It's my first day."
and, "I think I'm supposed to train with you."
I said, "Are you the Michael Fay from the news?"
He affirmed this with a sense of bored pride.

They caned him 4 times (reduced from 6).
I asked, "What are you doing in Minnesota?"
He said, "Going to treatment (at Hazelden)
for sniffing glue" (technically Butane).

He seemed to walk around like normal, but
he was a lousy worker—apathetic and slow.
I don't think I really said anything else to him,
and he never returned for a second shift.

That's the end of the story. I never saw him again.
There's no real point other than you never know
who you might run into next. And bussing tables
is a great deal harder than it looks.

the trick is to keep your marriage fresh

we only have one bathroom
my wife and I
(it's been a struggle)
I take long showers
so courtesy is key

just for instance
I used to say:
"do you need the bathroom before I shower"
but that got old day-after-day and
a good husband strives
to keep a marriage fresh, so I
started getting clever:

"do you need the splash-basket
before I shower?"

and

"need anything from the water closet
before I clean myself?"

and

"do you need the liquid laboratory
before I start my experiments?"

and

"do you need to make any wishes

before I dance in the fountain?"

and

"do you need the blessing box
before I get baptized?"

and

"do you need the plumbing laboratory
before I stand under the leak simulator?"

I'm in a tough spot
I shower every day
our marriage is still new
and I am running out
of clever words and clever ways
to say:

"I love you and
what's mine
is yours."

career advances

I hate the word *career*
a nasty word I slap away.
a word with no pranks.
a word with no play.
it sounds like *careen*
which means to go swift,
uncontrolled in some way.
it sounds just how a leprechaun
might say *q-ueer*.

it softens resolve.
it swallows ideals.

career should be a cuss!
it's decoration for dying.
it's transaction-branding—
"I promise to become this
if you promise to give that."

CA-REER
the sound of angels
crying

CA-REER
making us numb,
local, and fat.

CA-REER
amplifying sham

patriotism.

CA-REER
making us smart
about dumb things.

the wake

I worked with this guy
don't remember his name
who had financial plans

> *my last check was two grand*
> *but if I do double shifts*
> *throughout the weekend*
> *my next will be three*

and

> *I use my Gold Card*
> *to earn point rewards*
> *then transfer all that*
> *to my Platinum Card*

and

> *maxed out my Roth*
> *to reduce long-term tax*
> *obligations*

and

> *I buy my toilet paper*
> *in bulk at Costco*
> *get it for half the cost*

it gets hard for me to pay
attention for very long
if I can be honest with you
I sort of daydream
in his direction
while he blathers on

"What's so funny," he asks

shaking me loose
from my ponder
I'd been imagining
his funeral wake
(I know I know—not very polite)
I imagined it going down
in some grandiose chapel—
pews packed with people
in polished shoes
and black dresses
all eyes daydreaming toward
an ostentatious coffin
glossy and ornate and lavish
while one sad dope after another
took their turn at the podium
saying pleasant things
but not one of them able
try as they might
to remember his name

lightbulbs

we have a trillion lightbulbs,
a hundred different sizes.
fragile little heads housing
blazing illuminations.

trillions of lightbulbs all
connected to our switches,
spread out upon our grids.

we have so many lightbulbs
it's hard to see the stars
(except the really bright ones).

endless lightbulbs living,
countless lightbulbs dead
(crunching in our landfills,
crackling in our bins).

we have a trillion lightbulbs
to write our poems at night,
to reveal all of our dangers,
to illuminate our sinning.

we have so many lightbulbs,
and yet the dark is winning.

couch slouchers

we're both slouched
on the couch
missing
our dog.

it's been over a year—
almost two, in fact.

he should be over here
laying
on my right
resting
against my arm
and my thigh.

we're planning
soon
to get a new
dog,
but
our hearts still beat
in rhythm with the one
we lost.

we slouch here holding
one another's hands.

the television screensaver
clicks on,
leaves fall outside

the window,
the dryer moans
as laundry tumbles
in the heat and
a button or zipper
ticks and clicks
with each hot turn,
a disturbed clock
keeping the time
and rolling it out
to dry.

labor pains and pivot points

everyone's hustling to sell a book
panhandlers on the web
giving everyone the look
desiring disciples
fishing for followers
desperate shepherds
in need of sheep
pseudo-C.S.-Lewis's
recycling dull theologies

and here I come with my own book
which I know you'll really like
but it's so damn hard to get
an eye or audience
when everyone's got
a megaphone

there's so much noise
we've all gone deaf
now no one has an ear to hear
now a writer has no chance!

so that's why I
am done with words
and only speak
from this point forth
in sign language or
interpretative dance

"Never fly straight and level for more than 30 seconds in the combat area."

Adolph Malan,
pilot in the Royal Air Force, fought in the Battle of Britain. This quote comes from number 7 on Malan's Ten Rules for Air Fighting.

the art of conversation

I stomped off the snow
at this locally owned
coffee cafe,
went to the counter
ordered a joe.

some clever young dope
sat stoned at each table,
peering deep into the glow
of laptops, ipads, mobile phones.

the whole crowd sat drugged
on self-subsumed silence,
such that you
could hear the dude
in the back room
wash ev'ry spoon.

it would've been sad
if not for two old timers talking
under the clock
in the booth over beside
the picture window.

these two guys were loud,
in their eighties at least,
talking over coffee
and waffle plates.

the scrawny guy

told his big diabetic friend
all about his wife's
brand new hearing aid.

as he spoke, his chin
floated just barely above
the table edge.

time and circumstance
had wrecked his posture,
but had not hindered
his ability to tell
a story.

I forget much of what he said,
but I remember his lament:
"I dropped five grand
on a machine smaller than
a damned walnut."

the big guy replies:
"my first house
cost five grand!"

"don't I know it,"
cried the scrawny guy,
hands to the sky.

but he confessed
to desperation,
sick, I guess,

of his wife
saying over and over again:

what? what? what?

"so there it is.
now she can hear
everything I say."

the big guy
sort of pointed his fork
from his fist.
"so now she can tell you
what to do and what
you're doing wrong,"
he replied.

then, without missing a beat,
followed that up
with this clever gem:

"you didn't buy your wife
a hearing aid
you bought yourself
a supervisor."

they both let loose
with laughter.

then the big guy took

a turn, telling about
his war platoon, and about
trying to find strippers
in a foreign land
for a buddy's birthday
when none of the men
knew the language.

I couldn't catch
the details, but it involved
interprative dance and
it seemed like quite
a terrific,
hilarious
tale.

meanwhile,
the herd of pixel-pushing mutes
sat mesmerized by
glowing retina slabs
of various sizes.

I slammed back the last
drop of coffee from
my cup,
sad
for the death
of conversation,
the death of story telling.

the two old guys
stood to leave,
same as me,
but moved slower and
far less steady,
each man boasting
his own
idiosyncratic walk —
creative accommodations
to the pains and breakdowns
of prolonged age.

but they made their way
and I
slowed my pace
as they ambled past
each hypnotized bore.

and, as they approached me, I
held open the door.

epistemic evolution

facts are fun to bend
for a precious cause
or some financial end

reality seems malleable
(and fantasy is valuable)
in our euphoric youth

but in due time
facts go straight
and ears distrust
what they are told

the magic fades
as we get old

the lies grind down
innocense and
vitality

we gain a taste
for proof
and always come
to need
in due time
the truth

pizza boy

got my first real job
when I was twelve
though I had to lie
and tell them I
was thirteen

I answered phones
pizza place South
of the river
"Dominoes Pizza
this is Dan
we deliver"

we'd get real busy
then we'd get lulls

the delivery drivers
would smoke
sometimes cigarettes
sometimes something more
and some would drink
from flasks or
concoctions mixed
in soda bottles

in the summer I could stretch
the phone cord way out
to the side door
so I could hear it ring
from the parking lot

out back
and I'd hang out
with the drivers
throw the football around
or they'd play me music—
whatever they were in to
on their cassette players
in their crappy cars

like this one guy
he was really in to a
Milwaukee band
called The Violent Femmes
and this other driver
she introduced me to
Metallica

other times the drivers
would tease me
say it was past my bedtime
or they'd ask me if
I was getting any action
with the girls at school

they'd get a real thrill
out of making me blush
and I'd stand back there
under the moon and
stars and before their
old wise eyes feeling

like they could see
right through me

I was too young
to see through them
I mean
I couldn't really see
their woes

most of them were
druggies
burn-outs
deadbeats
dropouts
bores

but to little ol' me
not quite thirteen
they were shepherds
guiding as I stepped
just a little bit
—not too far—
into a strange
wide open
pasture

distracted driving

I text while I drive
I know it is wrong
but I'm still alive
and still going strong
going on forty-five

the road is long
so very long
and yet I arrive
like a catchy old song
played loud at some dive
it doesn't belong.

poem for the birds

we fold up the chairs,
shake off the sand,
make our way through
the bustling beach,
march toward the bar,
as the sun gets shy
behind a girthy cloud,
and the waves rub
against the shore
in a slow-motion
stutter.

some fat kid runs loud,
chasing a panicked seagull.

this kid, I can tell,
he's a real prick,
in his little fat-boy shorts
and untucked shirt,
chasing a harmless bird.
and as he chases,
he hollers out
some incoherent rage:
"GETAWK-BODAYOY!"
and the befuddled bird
scurries off with a squawk
and with its wings
half-spread.

then B stops and she

looks right at the kid:

"Hey! Stop that!"

the kid stands straight,
spins around to look at B.
I just watch the little prick—
I've been watching him
my whole life.
cocky.
braggadocios.
oppositional.
everything he breaks
pumps air into his ego.
everyone he hurts
becomes an ottoman
for his feet.

he locks eyes with B,
and asks, with his little
ringing voice, a voice
that's never been without,
that's never known
self-doubt, that's always gotten
whatever thing it wants,
a voice that's never had to pay
its dues, and with that voice
he asks B,
"Why?"

B retorts:
"because it's rude."

the chubby kid then looks
at the bird, then looks
away, perhaps for mom
or dad, but then, looking
back at B, he simply says:
"okay," then walks away.

we drop our chairs
outside the the place
and make our way
up to the bar.
I order the fish tacos.
B decides to try
the swordfish.

vagabond heart

I stood staring into the linen closet
calculating how soon I'd have to buy
more toilet paper

and it struck me that
Frédéric Chopin
had been dead
about 170 years

there still hasn't come
one single piano composer
better than Chopin

not even one

after all these years

not even close

that's gotta be tough
I mean for modern composers
especially competitive ones

also—and this is a true
story—the thought
of being buried alive
terrified Chopin

he reached up
from his bed

pulled the nurse near
and whisper-mumbled
in her ear

"have my heart
cut from my chest
before the shovel
hits the dirt"

and when he died
they complied
removed his heart
per his request
and sent it back
to what became
Poland

this was harder than
it sounds
they had to smuggle
Chopin's heart
through hostile Russia
—a land with no ear
for genius
it would appear

the heart now sits
sealed up high

on some shelf
in a jar of Cognac

Chopin's drunk heart
floats there in gold
amber fluid
a thousand miles
from his body

anyway
we had plenty of toilet paper
at least a couple weeks worth
"we should be fine" I said
as I closed the closet door

.

drowning at a baptism

oatmeal is good for the heart

it was early.
I was sleepy.
you were flirty.
I tried to scoop
the oatmeal flakes
into my empty bowl.
you were casting eyes,
steeping your tea,
and teasing me,
for what?
I don't recall.
"dang," I exclaimed,
"I've lost count of my scoops."
that's when you
looked down like you do
at my heaping bowl.

"how many scoops
do you usually use?"

I shrugged and said:

"two."

this time of year I crave junk food

gnats flap like mad
as hell inhales
heat retreats
the wind stings
icicles appear
on the puppeteer's
puppet strings
the last bird
without sound
flies slow
above the steeple
the ground
goes flat
and hard
people
grow round
and fat
while earth
somehow
still turns
with breath
so cold
it burns

The Olive Grove

my feet crunch dull
trodden snow
the wind blows cold

the sky above
a weak and dim
closed mouth

the earth
a stained off-white
rotted tooth

there's a Van Gogh
down in South
Minneapolis

sitting on a museum
wall for anyone to see
"The Olive Grove"

I remove my mittens
and my hat as I come in
to stand before it

my world freezes
Van Gogh's world melts
within that frame

his sun pets treetops
massages mountains
tickles grass

his sky stirs
and everything's
connected

I'm not a thief
wouldn't dream
of stealing

but after hours
I want to break in
with a crowbar

the painting
belongs right where it is
but the frame…

no masterpiece
ought to bear such burden
especially a Van Gogh

a frame obfuscates
a frame suffocates the fire
I want to destroy it

remove that sad
art condom and show me
its naked sides

show me where
illusion meets
reality

show me that thin portal
where his vivacious world
connects to mine

that I might find
a way to crawl
up inside

and feel that heat
from that light
for just a while

safe driver

I'm in my forties now
I wear my seatbelt
behind the wheel
look both ways twice
before crossing traffic
stay in the slow lane
let the speeders pass me by

when I was young
I'd challenge everyone
I sped and weaved
in-and-out of cars
took too many chances
even when the roads were iced
(several times I almost died)

the police wrote me tickets
revoked my license
but I'm still alive
and if my younger self
could see me now
he'd scoff and roll his eyes
at how dull I've become
behind the wheel

he'd think my fear of dying lame
he'd think my cautions dumb
he'd assume that I was soft
but he would be way wrong

we are in the heat of war
politicians mock our gods
(they hijack our beliefs)
product-pushers distort desires
(we buy the dumbest things)
industry destroys the earth
(we chip apart mountains
for fancy kitchen countertops
to butter bagels on)
hunters destroy every precious thing that moves
(we're running out of elephants)

I latch my seatbelt
slowly back out of the drive
there's a great many things
for which I could lay down
my life

and I'll be damned
if I'm giving mine
to save a minute
getting to a mall
or to avoid being late
to a job

in June grass grows fast
sunshine and rain baptize earth
damn this lawnmower

A MESSAGE TO
SO GREAT A CROWD...

...SO FAR AND SMALL BENEATH
YOUR FEET.

lesser drugs

uncle Casey made me laugh so hard
when I was a kid
I'd cry

one time we were laughing
I couldn't even breathe

another time in the truck
we made Grandpa mad
"Dammit I'm tryna' drive"
(but pretty soon he was laughing too)

Casey
he showed me treasures of humor
and joys hidden all around
and happiness I didn't even know
at that young age
could be found

he got married
became a dad
one night he got high
I think it was cocaine
hung himself
died

I was only a boy
I didn't understand
(I still don't)
there's no way cocaine

could feel like we felt
when we were laughing
side-by-side
in the front seat of grandpa's truck

there's no drug like us

if I could go back
I'd demand answers
and
I wouldn't even laugh
until I was
satisfied

kissing research

as a young man
when kissing a gal
I kissed too hard—
I'll be honest.

I'd press my lips
with great force
and enthusiasm
right against hers.

it felt real good
but also hurt—
I could feel the bone
above her teeth.

I take the blame
but dumb media
and inept metrics
were also at fault.

they led me to think
the silliest things:
passion is measured
somehow in pressure.

but then I got wise
softened my press
kissed her lips gently—
to astounding success.

two faces

I'll be sitting there
eyes fixed at passer-bys
at the mall or wherever
and, well, I just stare.
sorry if this creeps you out,
but what can I say?
people are, sometimes,
just so beautiful to me—
different colors of skin,
different types of hair,
each one a masterpiece
carved from marble,
or buffed from soapstone,
like they're meant to be
just how they are
(none of it wrong,
even their flaws)
and God is great
and eternity
is not too long.

but then these other times
(I don't know why),
something happens in my eye.
even pretty folks
look ugly, misshapen,
dull, un-sanctified—
greasy teeth, bulgy eyes,
mouths like fish and lips
smack saliva sounds and

evolution's cruel and slow
and life is an unsightly show.

I close my eyes.
I look away.

but age, I think,
makes one wise.
I wait it out
knowing that,
given time,
it will reverse,
and beauty will
return again,
and so will youth—
and someday
stay for good—
and the lies
of ugliness
will finally die
forever—

assuming, of course,
that beauty is
the truth.

The Idea of Light:

The Bible starts with poetry
God hovering over the deep
The idea of light kneeling at God's feet
Begging God for actuality
God considers light's plea
Utters his decree:

Let There Be...

the comedian

it was early
B and I out on the deck
eating oatmeal
drinking tea

a woodpecker kept pulling back
her pompous head
way far back
then she'd slam
her face
into a dead tree trunk

again and again
and we'd laugh

then the dizzy bird
would rest
sip her latte
then resume her brutal task

she slammed
and slammed

and slammed
again

the trees were cartoon
green and the sky glowed
blue and sunny
in late July

we were amazed and
feeling lucky

life can be a splendid show
and God
is funny

I'm not yet who I want to be

I devour frozen burritos
especially these tofu ones—
I buy 'em by the case

so I have this cardboard box
when the burritos are gone
can't bring myself to throw it away
(it's the perfect size
for something)
for now it waits
on the top shelf
of my book case

today I was cleaning
pulled the box down
a little spider made a home
in a lower corner
he seemed friendly enough
but I didn't much appreciate him
doing his creepy business
so very close to where
I do my sacred work

yet it was too cold
to let him outside
(negative thirty windchill)
so I passed down my verdict:
  execution-by-thumb-press

I grabbed a tissue

(who wants spider-guts
all over their fingers?)
and I pressed down
and felt his body crunch
beneath my caped thumb

I shivered off the wicked act
but when I raised my hand
the little fighter resumed his crawl
I struck again as he dashed
under a cardboard flap
after a couple more
maddening attacks
I finally conquered him
pinched his carcass
into the tissue shroud
(his white burial cloth)
dabbed-up his guts
from off the box
set the tissue in the trash

I put the box
back on the shelf

someday I'll need it
it's the perfect size
for something

heaven, expectations of

as the years go by
my expectations
for heaven
diminish

my younger self
demanded health
epic adventure
to be entertained

daydreams of heaven
involved visions of sky-diving
racing on unicorns
dancing with damsels
things like that

but as the years pass
a simple field of grass
my wife in her chair
right over there
my dog sniffing a breeze close by
enjoying olfactory treasures
we can't even see

my wife and my dog and me
in creation redeemed
this describes in full
all that I would need

improbable win

in the summer as a boy
I'd go up north
to my grandparent's cabin
up in Hackensack
Minnesota

sometimes we'd go to auctions
marvelous auctions
grandpa bought me hot dogs
and root beer
then he'd bid on chainsaws
and wheel barrows
kerosene lamps
and mechanical cuckoo clocks
and sometimes he'd bid
on a miscellaneous box

these boxes would have
maybe one or two good things
like a hunting knife
or a novelty shoe horn
and it would be in a box
with gads of other junk

this one time grandpa bid
because he wanted a fishing reel
and he won and he took the reel
and gave what was left to me
I scored a dozen
brand new tennis balls

bright and green
and six or seven
long and finely sanded
ergonomic wooden
axe handles

I was thrilled and knew
just what I could do

the axe handles
would be golf clubs and
all those tennis balls
would be golf balls
I made a sprawling
championship golf course
all throughout grandpa's property
with empty coffee cans for holes
buried up to their open rims

I'd play these epic tournaments
for ten hours a day
I'd play and play and play
I hit some incredible shots
under tremendous pressure
against Hall of Fame opponents

and after each breathtaking win
I'd have colorful interviews

with CBS and ESPN
and I'd explain to them
each important shot
of my improbable win
until the sun would dip down
below the tree tops
and grandpa or grandma
would call me back in

in the end the jesters win

I didn't even hear him knock
he stood there with his coat
staring at my front door
with fat mittens and
a black leather
portfolio book

I swung open the door
and said "what's up?"

"helloooooooo," he said
with a cheer
and terror
you'd see in a court jester
trying to convince a king
not to behead him

"is this a good time to talk
about retirement planning?"

it wasn't

I removed my reading glasses
and looked him in the eyes
"dude you were already here"

"that's right" he said
"just last summer" and
"you have a great memory"

believe me I felt for the guy—
selling retirement planning
door-to-door and all—but
it was only twelve degrees outside
and I was in my boxer shorts
and in the middle of writing
a tricky transition sentence

"just give me your card" I said
then did the little give-it-here wave

he extracted one carefully from his portfolio
then reached it out to me
I took it
mumbled a good-bye as I
pushed the door shut
with the heel of my foot

I did read his card—
he'd earned that—
on my way back
to my writing desk

      J... Colby
      Financial Advisor

there will come a day
I just know it
when I will painfully regret
my reckless disdain

for financial planning

but at that moment
as I sat back at my desk
I saw him slogging up
and down the neighbors
drive

and I was holding his card
a inch or so above the shredder
his picture pinched under my thumb
and I released the card
into the gears and proclaimed:

"Off with his head!"

the fundamentals of being myself

be yourself!
be yourself!
they say,

just be yourself!

on every shirt,
in every song,
on every book,
on every day.

be myself, huh?

no thanks!

I've been myself
all my whole life.
here, YOU be me
for a while,
then we'll see
who really truly wants to be
themselves

we simply cannot divorce ourselves

people do whatever
they must do
I guess

I'm sure they do
just look at them

they take these jobs
or start these careers

excitement builds
as does dread

the money helps
but also hurts

they feel alive
but also dead

the work gets bigger
and starts to collapse
down and around
their vital self

they draw a line
they fight to guard their hearts
from the toil
of it all

"it's not me," they say,

"I just do this
to pay the bills."

and I know how good
it feels
to pay the bills

you're a king
or a queen
when you pay the bills
solving problems
meeting needs
issuing your decree
with button clicks
and written checks
or credit card
swipes

it feels so good
it feels so right
to build your kingdom
stone-by-stone

then comes promotion
extra courses
double shifts

that part of you
the part you guard
forgets who it was
loses voice

loses direction
loses choice

career
gets bigger
louder
more and more
important

and then you meet up
with a friend
from back in the day
at Starbucks
and you say "hey"
and smile all over
and get your coffee drink

I'm at the table over here
working on a thing
watching you sit
across from your friend

I listen in
for a bit

the two of you laugh
"it's been so long"

but the only thing
you talk about
is work

and the hours
and the toil
and the drama
and the importance
of your place

I place my headphones
over my ears
where masters bathe me in cellos
and violins
to block you out
because
well
I do not mean to offend
but I don't know you and
you bore me

I've lost interest in you
and your story
and don't care how
it all will end

and as you disappear from me
I notice
you've also lost the interest
of your friend

the witness

did you see that spider?
did you see how big he was?
when I saw him I was sitting
right here in this coffee shop
sipping a creamy latte
thinking about the goodness
of God's creation when my eye
caught something unholy crawling
so I turn my head to the left
gazed through this window here
(close enough for me to touch)
and there upon that outside wall
I saw the dark and tentacled beast
rising smoothly up concrete
in his complicated strut
pure horror on the move
making his repugnant way
up up up through his busy day
somewhere between his vicious tasks
disappearing and reappearing
in-and-out of gaps and cracks
depleting creation's goodness
right out there in my world
on the other side of the glass
well within my reach but
just outside my grasp

"In combat flying, fancy precision aerobatic work is really not of much use. Instead, it is the rough maneuver which succeeds."

Erich Hartmann,
the most successful fighter ace in the history of aerial warfare. Learned to fly from his mother.

sips

sirens in the distance
the cops are on the search
people flood the coffee shop
the coffee shop is church
the traffic never stops
the sheep are in a trance
hypnotized with Starbucked eyes
tattoos and saggy pants
shirts untucked with comfy shoes
some are reading Twitter
some are reading news

coffee cups go up and down
from tabletops to lips
some are jolly some are bitter
some are fatter some are fitter
some are leaving tips
each one dumb to consequence
their folly and their fritter
the froth of lifelong choices made
each choice just like a sip
they come in vans and trucks and cars
buying beverages and sweetened breads
oblivious to their progress bars
that only God and I can see
floating just above their heads

muse funeral

I get like this
late-night-nothing-stare
my wife's in bed and I
should be there
too
but feel
like I'm supposed to wait

for what
I don't know
I listen to music
I sip my drink

I wait
it's almost midnight
I wait
and wonder
if angels can die
I wonder
if muses can die
and how would I know
if it happened
to mine?

eyes of the machine

it happens wherever
we go, it seems,
in every part of the world,
but it really got to me in this great old castle
in the city of Prague,
year of our lord
twenty-sixteen.
it was me and B
and hordes of folks
like slow-motion cattle
pushing slowly through
the ancient complex.

what struck my anger:
every site seer took pictures
of every silly thing.

they took pictures of the ceiling,
the gargoyle statues,
the walnut pews,
the traffic stanchions,
a painting of John the Baptist having
a deep thought,
that statue of Mary doting
on her child,
a stained glass window showing
soldiers slaying soldiers
for some small cause.

iphones cameras ipads

snapping pictures just because.
snapping pictures in all the halls.

they took pictures of the doors,
the stairs,
the floors,
a sink.
they took pictures of
their shoes,
their moods,
some even took a picture
of other people taking pictures.

my mind got tight with dread
and I pushed to find a place
to think.

can't we simply use our eyes
to look at all the things?

must we each upload
and archive
every single thing
we see?

apparently not.

no no no
we must upload each scene,
for we are now, each of us,
the indentured eyes

of the great online machine.

hundreds thousands millions
of pictures taken
of the same dumb things.
and you know damn well,
when they show their pictures
to their family,
to their coworkers,
to their hostages,
to their friends,
they'll end up saying
the same damn thing:

"the photo doesn't do it justice," and,
"you just had to be there."

but none of them were there.
only B and me,
getting jostled through
the maddening crowd
of the machine's
brain-washed
paparazzi.

evidence that demands a verdict

Barbara bought the toilet paper last.
she bought the good stuff.

firm. soft. heavy.

many times her frugality
guides her eye and hand,
and many times
the less expensive brand
ends up in her cart.

she's visiting friends in Milwaukee right now,
so I can't thank her.

no, I'm sitting here several
hundred miles away.

alone.

I know guys who would mope
if their woman leftthem like this.
they'd feel unloved, abandoned,
rejected.

I reach over and grab a couple
pillowy squares off the roll.

I don't have to worry
about anything like that.

my birthday falls in March

I was born on the brink
of spring
and every year
it's the same old thing
the frozen ground
dissolves to slop
the winter witch
escapes upon
a soppy mop
and birds return
to chirp and squawk
and smiling geese
come home
in flying Vs
to poop on all our lawns
while maple trees
ooze with sap
to nourish embryonic leaves
and I complete
another lap
with smiling emojies
in my hands
LOL emojies
up my sleeves

flight dreams

I've had flight dreams
they come to me
most often when life dances
exactly how I want it to

during these good times
in my life
I'll dream I can fly
without help from jets
planes
catapults
or any other human device
nothing but my own robust
will
guided only by my eyes
and mind

I simply look up to where
I want to be
then I zoom on up
through the air
to the spot

simple as that

what interests me most
about these flight dreams
this ability to fly
comes as a surprise
and almost always when

I am alone

it comes to me
as an epiphany
like I will stand
in some old alley
or walk on through
some empty barn
without a crowd
or even a person
anywhere around

then I'll get this sense
and so I try
then to find

 I CAN FLY!

and I'll lift off
easy and light
with no one else around

you might think I'd want
a witness
someone to see
such an amazing feat
and I do normally enjoy
attention

but when I fly

in these dreams
I don't want others to know

I hide

even when I see the folks
walking around below
I fly over them real still
and even hold my breath

I think what it is
even in my dream
I know
if I could fly
and if others were around to see
at first they'd be surprised
and maybe want a ride

but then
soon after
these ground walkers
these dirt huggers
these hopelessly lowly folks
if they were around
to see from the ground
even in my dream
I know
they would try
to pull
me down

social media

numb

brains

f l o a t i n g

gently

down

algorithmic

content

streams

fog on bridges

the bridge to the past
disappears
into a fog
of the heart

you step onto that bridge
you move into that fog
you walk
and walk
and walk

but always arrive
wherever
you start

4

smooth jazz
for martyrs

me on my bike

on my bike I test
the myths
of physics

leaning

turning

fast

faster

weight and inertia
pulling me
this way and that
until
a weight drops off
deep inside
like a wet robe

and

I feel like a boy
again
dumb to the wonders of
maturity

master only of balance and
being easy
to please

the ones that work

I write lots of these poems
most of them duds
they just don't work
don't play
don't dance

I try to fix them
to no avail
the verse stays flat
my tricks all fail

but sometimes my tricks succeed
I change a word
remove a line
figure it out
and
resurrection occurs

T R A N S F I G U R A T I O N

man those are the good ones

but the best ones
(and they're rare)
are poems that work
just as they come
and I have no idea why
or how
or from where

the goons will come to collect

the sleep was good
that's the thing
I was on my belly
left leg extended
right leg out
bent at the knee
like it was resting on a fence
in some fantastic dream
my blanket poured over me
lightly so I wasn't sweating
heavy so I wasn't insecure
my feet poked out the edges
to dispense my excess heat
a breeze blew summer colors
through the window screen

I lay unconscious in the calm
and my pillow held my head
like a mother holds a child
like a preacher holds a Psalm
it was a drunken sleep
it was a healing sleep
it was
a stolen sleep
embezzled from some cosmic mob
who'd now sent their goons in black
to reclaim what I had taken
just after 6:30 in the morning

they taunted me from the street
barking alarming shrieks
like circus clowns being choked
like party horns from hell
like pterodactyls being poked
I tried to sleep through
but they refused to stop

  ACK! ACK! ACK! ACK! ACK!

they bullied me until
I went downstairs to confront them
out the front door
across the cold lawn
drowsy and mad

there were two in the street
and even more in the trees
dressed in black suits with black hoods
I flailed my arms on approach
and hollered some desperate nonsensical
incantation
and when they saw me awake
they knew they'd acquired
what they'd been sent there to take
so they finally took flight
(first the two in the street
then a hundred more
from who knows where)

when I was sure they were gone
I turned back to my home
scratching my ass
bare-foot on the lawn
on wet morning grass
in only my boxers and tee

I looked up at my room
stretching and yawning
and considered how far
from my cozy night sleep
I had fallen

caught up in hypothetical moments

I have all these questions
for God

questions questions questions

the point of it all
what causes evil
the truth about Jesus
the point of me
and so forth
and so on

but

if I were ever to stand
before the Creator
under the awe
and the staggering glow
I'm sure I'd get
swept up in that presence
and tensions deep inside
would release
tensions
I never even knew I had

and I'd laugh
and I'd listen
and I'd relax

and

all those questions
well
knowing me
I'd forget
to ask

my new hat

got me a new hat
a wicker thing
sort of a cross between
a cowboy and
safari hat

it's purely functional
not for fashion

but I like the straw color
and how it curls up
slight on the sides
and then curls down
slight on the front

it fits me alright
but it's just for function
not for looks

I've got this skin
condition and
the hat
it blocks the sun
from my ears
and face

but I like how I
can grab the top
pinch a little
lift it up from my hair

to say, *hello there*

or I can take it off
and press it soft
over my heart
if there's a moment
of silence or
maybe an anthem
or some other
sentimental
thing

it has three breathe holes
to keep my head
from overheating
and a chocolate colored
racing band
for style

but this hat here
it's not for style
it's for function

like say for instance
I piss off a dangerous snake
and let's just say he's posturing
like he wants to strike
well I'm not sure
but

I bet I could trick the viper
into attacking my hat
instead of me
if I held it out in front
in just the right way

it's a good hat
and
there are many things
it can do
especially for
the right man

I'm thinking
here
for instance
a man
of adventure
such as
myself

trembling

trembling, I ran a trembling
finger across the trembling
page of some trembling
poet's book of trembling
poems

until I came to that trembling
word I can't tolerate: *trembling*
trembling trembling trembling
whenever I read *trembling*
I shudder

there are synonyms for trembling
so if you still overuse trembling
maybe you should go trembling
into something other than trembling
into poetry

the day I met Arnold Palmer's nephew

I was at this bar
just me and two black guys
sitting there
New Tampa Florida
watching Golden State take it to
some inferior basketball team

on this one play
Steph Curry drained
a wide-open
three-point
shot
and the skinny black guy
at the end of the bar
looked at me then looked
at the big black guy next to him and said

"they got what they deserved there
that's just what they get
doubling Cousins like that"

I pointed a hand at the TV
"Curry's gonna drain that shot
all day and all night"

they both nodded and offered
Mmm-Hmms and *that's-rights*

those guys were just what I needed
and I was so glad they were at the bar

I was beginning to think
the population of Tampa
consisted only of fat
white folks
like me

Curry stole the basketball
tossed it to Kevin Durant
who dashed to the hoop but
tossed it out to Clay Thompson
at the last second
who then drained yet another
wide-open
three-point
shot

"Man, you just gotta' foul KD
on that drive there" said
the big black guy and
"Warriors just toying with 'em now"

then Golden State had such a large lead
a lead too big to lose
so the coach sent in some backup players
and that's when I thought about
leaving

* * *

here's something true about me
I want black men to like me

not that I prostrate myself
at their feet
or smile like a dope
for no reason
whenever they're around
I just long for these
connections
these
shared moments
that might build
bridges
for greater things like
say
the miracle
of reconciliation

* * *

the two guys settled their checks
with the bartender
and were about finished
with their beers when
this smiley white guy with his gal stepped up
and sat at the bar and I
just knew the vibe
would die

"Guess how much a ticket
to the Master's Tournament
practice is" the white guy asked
in the direction of

the black guys

"I bet it's a lot" the big black guy said
in his slow casual voice

"almost a thousand dollars"
said the white guy "just
to watch a practice"

the goof must've been very impressed
with this fact because
he repeated it again
and again

then as they were leaving
the big black guy
points
to the skinny black guy
and says
"RJ here is Arnold Palmer's
nephew"

the white guy sat straight
and blinkless
"WOW that's amazing"

big black guy then gives me
a laughing glance
as he leaves the bar

* * *

the whole scene then became a bore
I waved for my check

that's when this new black guy
with a woman
steps up and sits
in the vacated seats

"these open" he asks

white guy says "yep"
and "Arnold Palmer's nephew
was just sitting there"

the black woman was
hanging her purse on the
chair

white guy sat there looking
at black guy who
simply opened his menu
which covered most of his face
then replied with a bored
and simple

"uh-huh"

the Kingdom of Darkness advances one software update at a time

not too long ago
when you'd visit friends
and hang out at their houses
and when conversation
waned
they'd get up
and leave the room

then they'd return
with photos
in an album
in a stack
or in a shoe box
and they'd show you
pictures

looking at all these pictures was toilsome
but
you'd tolerate it because
well
they were your friends and
you cared about them and
you liked hanging out
with them

now
thanks to blessed technology
and the miracle of social media
all we get are the pictures
and we never hang out

the school

sometimes I like to test myself
like I'll piss in the bathroom
with the lights off
trusting only in my aim
oriented in the dark
by the trash can here
and the edge of the rug
there

or sometimes I'll take note
when I'm out-and-about
all around town
of fantastic places to hide
if the need should arise

or cozier places to sleep
should my life fall apart
like under that bridge
or up on that roof of that old
shopping mart

or sometimes when I buy
a cart full of groceries
I'll carry it all out to my truck
without using a bag
dozens of things in a bundle
with bananas under an arm
bread dangling from my hand
frozen vegetables up
on my shoulders and down

in my pants

or sometimes when I drive
with an elbow on the wheel
and one eye on the road
I'll eat a sandwich
while listening to a podcast
and typing a buddy a text

I run myself through all
varieties of drills
and experiments

because life is an unpredictable school
and you just never know what
it will test you on
next

Rockstar Epistemology

I was doing godly stuff
at this ministry place,
doing good works, like—
well, I don't recall just now, but
I'm sure soup was involved.

anyway, I got dragged in to some
conversation about God
with this scrawny,
rockstar looking kid—
barely old enough to drink
(whose worldview led him
to an early meth addiction
and a body and face full
of tattoos and piercings,
just like every rockstar
on every music magazine
and music video at that time).

he approaches me and says something
I've heard dozens of other tattooed,
scrawny, rockstar kids say,
he says:

Christians are just
mindless,
brainwashed,
obedient sheep.

existential immunity

maybe it's my age
(I'm getting old)
but all the woe
from my road
(every unfair pain)
softens like the sun
at dusk
and decomposes
into black and white
movie scenes
in my brain —
scenes from a show
about some dope
I don't even know
anymore

all those electrified
barbed-wire
memories
don't affect me
all that much
like before

don't make me slouch
under their weight

don't even make me cry
(my eyes are dry)

I am a statue now

fully carved
by an unseen artist I hope to meet
some day

the stone is set
and sealed
and can't be carved
anymore

it can only be broken
down into dust
or persist
if it must
for others to see

I put the *can* in cannabis

I smoked pot.
just once.
out in Colorado, shortly after
they legalized it.

I know, I know, what a rebel, huh?
I guess it made me feel, well,
maybe a little more attentive.
I remember noticing great detail
in the woodgrain of the patio deck
and the eye-liner and pantyhose
of a chubby spider
dangling below
her horrific web.

but that's about it.
the pot didn't do
much else for me—
they say it can induce euphoria,
but, here's the thing:
for the most part, on my own,
I'm already a fairly euphoric guy.

listen,
I live in a state
with only six weeks of summer.
how else do you think
I get by?

how will the people ever hear the truth?

I was doing rounds,
up and down the hall,
with my clipboard
and flashlight.

I swung the light
into room 322 where
this wide-eyed woman
stood staring straight at me
from the darkness.

"Just doing rounds, Faith,"
I said, and marked the sheet.

"Do you want to see my stool,"
she asked with an air of pride.

"Is it in the toilet?"

"No, dear. I took it out.
I was concerned
because
it was hard."

"No-no," I said,
"I don't need to see it, I
trust you know
what you're talking
about."

"Yes I do, dear."
she was almost smiling.

I put the clipboard
under my arm
leaned to leave.

"Do you believe in God,"
she asked, with the delicate voice
of a grandmother
about to read
a bedtime tale.

"We don't talk about God
on the unit,
Faith,
sorry—unit rule."

"Oh, you don't, dear?
Are you Jewish? Pagan?
Buddhist?"

I thought maybe I could end
the conversation
through abstraction,
so I confessed, "No-no,
I'm a theist."

her face swelled
into a blinkless

horror-stare.
"You're ATHEIST!"

I did the calm-down thing
with my hands,
"No-no, I'm a
theist."

"Oh I *know* what
an atheist is!
I'm not talking
to you
anymore!"

Then she flicked
off the light
and slammed
the door.

once the crumbling starts it's hard to stop

mom told me she quit
smoking
again
it really does seem different
this time
but lately
well
lately I've been despairing death

not death
per se
more
the gradual destruction of God's good
creation
all the trash in the ocean
the disappearance of nature
the awful wrath of city planners
everything good being squeezed
to suckle the vigorous addictions
of the coddled masses

"I'm on my 10th day"
she says
and
"this time it's different"

it's hard to trust
even best
intentions
to change a habit

it goes against our nature
but I tell her I love her
and that she is worth
her effort
because
giving up
and
losing hope
also goes
against our nature

the machines must make you think they're people

machines call me all day long
and the machines are getting better
mailmen jam my box with junk
while no one writes a letter
robocalls and junk mail tactics—
they say I'm great but could be better
they say I'm weak but could be strong
and warn me that my life is wrong
they try to give my heart a scare
they warn me of asbestos death
and other toxins in the air
they warn of trouble from the IRS
and suggest I'm in an awful mess
they ask if I've insured my life
they worry what I'll leave my wife
they activate strategic tensions
and creep their schemes in dark dimensions

it's a numbers game—we're each a number
they want inside our leather wallets
they want for us to drop our guard
they want from us an open heart
the robocalls must sound like people
the envelopes must look hand-written
inside you floats a shiny nickel
you have to fight to keep it hidden

A Cheese Poem for Chesterton

"Poets have been mysteriously silent on the subject of cheese."
—G.K. Chesterton

Yes of course since
childhood
grilled cheese dipped
in tomato soup
the body and the blood
of toddler communion

"mommy says protein
is good for my growth"

later on pizza
all those toppings
melted mozzarella
unifying diversity

"teacher says calcium
is good for my bones"

and fancy sandwiches
as my appetites grew
with provolone
or cheddar
melted through
like a warm hug
on my inside
that God foreknew

I would need
to make me better
when I discover
the world is cold
and I am alone

then as aging kicks in
bleu cheese crumbles
sprinkled on salads
to satisfy
a lingering taste
for death
even while I try so hard
to prolong
my life

cheese cheese cheeses
it comforts and it pleases
it makes the blandest dishes
taste so darn divine
but revelation from
science's unfolding bible
reveals the truth

    it's all a lie

Satan has come
as an angel of light
seduced us with salt
and the creamiest fats

and made us believe
like Adam and Eve
that poison was fruit
and even good
for godly pursuit

but now we know better
from gouda
to cheddar

cheese arrives
fully disguised
as some kind of divine
kenosis—
but brings only metabolic
acidosis
and eventually
osteo-
porosis

a library of laments

everybody's handing me books
books they wrote
books they didn't
books with flaps
books with bows
books unwrapped
books about God
books inviting
books about dogs
books on writing
books on kenosis
some exciting
some laborious
everybody handing me books
but what I really need
is not another book
but time
to read

what are books, really?
mental obituaries
leather-bound tombstones

waterfowl

I was in the shower
rinsing off the soap.
you swung open
the bathroom door,
let out a giddy scream,
stepped into the steam.

"Oh my god! Oh my god!"
you exclaimed.

"what is it," I replied,
pulling back the curtain wide.

"Two big trumpeter swans
just flew over my head
back on the deck," you said,
and, "it was amazing.
they were enormous."

you were excited
and you looked
gorgeous.

and then you hopped
from one foot to the other,
head tilted back
shouting:

HONK! HONK! HONK!

arms out flapping,
water splattering
upon your sweater.
then you told me,
"I wish you'd seen it!"

I wished I did, too,
but in reality, I think,
what I saw from you
was far far better.

sounds of home

as I get older
the sounds of nature
the birds
the wind in trees
the frogs
the bees
the bugs
the dogs
it all sounds so sweet
to me

no more than static
to a child
I suppose
but I am not a kid and
as death sneaks near
these sounds get clear
comforting
they call to me like a friend

I feel these sounds
between my brain
and my heart
which pounds
as the gentle hands
of earth
surround me
and nurture me
day-by-day
chirp-by-chirp

breeze-by-breeze
and all that sings
prepares my body and blood
for my great return
home
to my rightful place
in things

the flash

Mike and I had this buddy Chad—
about as interesting as an elbow pad.
We hung out with him anyway
because his sister turned us on.

We'd go to Chad's house, over
by the grade school playground,
but we'd end up messing around
with his sister the whole time.

One night outside her bedroom window
Mike did a daring thing: he tapped and
tapped and tapped the glass and kept
tapping until she finally came.

She yanked open the curtains and stood
in pajamas she was too old for—
the buttoned kind that fit her whole body
with the foot coverings and all that.

"What do you perverts want? My dad
is going to kick your ass." Her words
were angry but her tone was not and
I stepped out of the dark to Mike's side.

She was older than us by a couple years
and looked more like a woman than
a girl and had breasts and she dated a
football player or secret agent or something.

"Show us your tits," Mike said and I
was appalled at his bold request—
yet I leaned away from the shadows
toward her outpouring bedroom light.

"I'm not showing you my boobs," she said,
because obviously she didn't want to and
for that reason I didn't want her to, either
—yet Mike and I kept inching closer.

"Oh come on," Mike pressed, and,
"How about just a peek for me."
He pleaded with tones and gestures
masterfully polished beyond his years.

He worked her to the point that she
unbuttoned her top and we could see
her skin all the way down to her belly
button—even between her breasts.

Earlier that day we had played
with G.I. Joe action figures and I
never anticipated seeing anything like
what stood before us just then.

But Mike was still not content and,
to close the sale, he made his final
pitch: "you show us your breasts,
then we'll show you our dicks."

"What makes you think I want
to see your little dicks," she said,
and I was relieved because she
was right about my little dick.

Then, as I was thinking about my
inadequacies, she grabbed the opening
of her pajama top and pulled apart
revealing everything to Mike and me—

then immediately covered up
again and everything revealed
was shrouded and there was a sense
that dramatic music had crashed to a stop.

But we both saw what there was
to see and it was marvelous even
to me, though I was too young
to comprehend really any reason why.

Our mouths hung open and then
she leaned toward us and gently said:
"Okay now you show me yours,"
and I was smacked with panic.

I hit my head on her open window
as I tried to turn and run away.
Then I collided with Mike who
was also turning to run away.

We leapt through her backyard
bushes, back into the grade school
playground—cowards on the run,
pseudo-Adams looking for cover.

Years later, as a man, I paid a visit
to Mike, who'd gained weight
and adopted a marijuana habit.
I asked whatever happened to her.

"She's a stripper at Deja Vu,"
he said, "Fridays and Saturdays."
Then he asked if I wanted to get
stoned and go see her show.

I thought back to her staring down
from her window, and Mike and I
staring up with dumbstruck eyes
at her tiny flash of sacred flesh.

She must've felt like a goddess who
could extract whatever she wanted
from so weak a world and from men
so obedient to her every whim.

But there's danger, too, I guess,
with power so easy to abuse, like
Elijah calling fire down from God
or Oppenheimer building bombs,

or Kurt Cobain writing songs.
we each could use some help
to hold each other down, so we
don't destroy each other or ourselves.

I zipped up my coat and said "no,"
put on my shoes to go and asked
at the door, "whatever happened
to Chad?" But Mike didn't know.

this is planet earth
feel free to look around folks
ev'rything's for sale

5

snow-boarding over bell-curves

Minneapolis Minnesota

behold the land
of frozen rivers
and falling bridges
of thinkers and givers
of poets and Princes

between the head
and the heart of our
blossoming nation
where every winter
tears us apart
and every spring
feels like salvation

how do we get out of this state?

heading back to Minnesota
back to hostile mosquitos
desperate to meet mad quotas
back to the torrid mania
of truncated summers
back through Madison
Baraboo
Black River Falls
and past a thousand carcasses
slaughtered by our auto cars
white-tails
raccoons
turtles
democrats
dragged to the side of the road
to rot before an audience of cars
heading back to Minnesota

where wind comes from

I used to think the leaves
bunched on the trees
created the wind

like I'd step outside
into the shine
the trees would see me
and they'd erupt
in greeting
crazy waving
saying hello

and their waving
pushed the air
down the streets
over the lawn
through my hair
across the skies

I used to think the leaves
made wind blow
and to tell you the truth
I've yet to find
convincing proof
it's otherwise

boy at the window

when I was a boy I'd fill up with sad
feel so alone
weep at my window

if Elon Musk ever gets
his shit together
and builds us a machine
for traveling in time
I'd go back
across all the decades back
past many heartbreaks back
beyond dumb investments back
before disappointments back
over all the carcasses of loved ones
slaughtered under cancer's killing spree

if I could time travel
I'd go back to me
at that window
and give me a hug
—or maybe I wouldn't
I can't decide—
but I'd look me right in the eye
and say

> *now is not the time*
> *to cry*
> *or fret*
> *stand up straight*
> *get tougher*

you haven't even begun
to suffer
yet

life's a beach alright
there's no lifeguard on duty
swim at your own risk

our backyard

is ample
almost an acre
with many trees

it stretches back
to a marshy pond

I look back there
and tell myself I'm looking
out into the wild
into God's untamed
marvel of nature

but this
for the most part
is a lie

I've neighbors to the left
I've neighbors to the right
and a neighbor on the other side
of the pond
the pond we can see
through barren branches
of winter light
and just past that
County Road C
then Maplewood Mall
and just past the city's edge
zoned land before another town
then more land where deer

are tagged and tracked
by government officials

I touch the window glass
of my patio door
bemoan the trees and grass
it's all a sham
not much more than office plants
that decorate a sad
cubicle cell
nature has been tamed
tagged and
contained

I someday want
somehow
to live at some edge
of some authentic wild
the edge of some wilderness
in which no one knows what lurks
and you can venture out for days
and never see a power line
and never see a city marker
and never climb an oil pipe
real nature that exists
just how it is
without our presence
without our permission
without our consent

playing with the locks

it's hard to eat steak
in front of a dog
and
you can't drive a new car
through the poor part of town
and
it's hard to be up
around those who are down

there's something inside
that binds us as one
the suffering of others
thwarts our own pleasure
and so heaven must be
where none of us suffer

and hell must be locked
from the inside as well
because I know that my wife
and my mom and my dog
and all of my friends
though they dwell up in heaven
and frolic with God
I have no doubt
they'll be woeful and sad
'til I find my way out

I'll get that to you by the end of business

responsibilities
and
obligations
tap on the glass

buzzers buzz
alert lights flash
in all their places

people wait
with pointed eyes
for me to push the finished task
before their faces

but I just stare
over my desk
thinking of my dog
we put to sleep last spring

he came to me last night
at the close of a vivid dream
and plopped down in the bed
beside my arm like he did

distressed clients send me texts
holler through their megaphones
drop fluttering flyers
from circling helicopters

but I just smile them off
not caring what they say
not sharing in their dread

instead
I caress the spot along my arm
where my dog in my dream
laid his head

diseased

apparently, to get a disease
established in the vernacular
you only need to make
a diagnosis.

every day I hear
a new one

greed is a disease
hate is a disease
addiction is a disease
and so forth

obesity
racism
social media
religion
atheism
liberalism
laziness
depression
all of them diseases
apparently

It's all ridiculous of course—
if everything's a disease, then nothing is—
but what do you do?

then earlier today I'm dabble-sucking
a macchiato at a coffee shop

checking the news feed on my phone

Hurricane Harvey baptized Houston with wrath
destroying cars, yards, homes, and plans, and
insurance loopholes mean 84 percent of those folks
won't be reimbursed
Trump pardoned some racist sheriff
a pregnant woman in Fargo was killed for her child
North Korea taunts the world with little missiles
housing costs soar
health care costs soar
bumble bees are disappearing
super bugs are becoming resistant to drugs
there are toxins in our drinking water
(the water in Flint Michigan remains undrinkable)
1 in 10 children will be sexually abused
a thousand elderly folks were scammed
out of their IRAs
Amur leopards are almost extinct
20 percent of the rainforest is now gone
a group of teens beat
a handicapped girl unconscious
temperatures will remain
below average until Monday

I take another sip and look around
the coffee shop where
some cartoonish woman sits
three tables over
life-coaching the shit out of her friend

"positivity trumps negativity" and
"stay away from all negative people" and
"you can't see shadows when
you're staring at the sun" and
"always look on the bright side—
surf optimism" and "you can't get positive
results from negative thoughts" and
"always smile—a positive attitude is contagious"
and on and on and on with her contrived and
discordant counsel while smiling like
a mannequin with puppet-eyes
while her friend smiles awkward
and checks the time

as for me I catch myself
with a look I'd call *aghast*
I reach for my pen
to scribbled out
my own diagnosis

HAPPINESS IS A DISEASE

...TO REMAIN OUT OF

THEIR REACH...

On the Geometry of Spirituality

I found myself on a spiral,
downward,
and this to me was fine.

I was glad to be off
the circle,
sliding around a different line—

because a circle, though level,
is infinite
and rides a redundant bend.

but the downward spiral
goes somewhere,
and often has an end.

"In the case of pilots, it is a little touch of madness that drive us to go beyond all known bounds. Any search into the unknown is an incomparable exploitation of oneself."

Jacqueline Auriol,
spent spent 3 years in the hospital recovering from a major crash, then returned to flight and broke several speed records. Divorced Paul auriol in 1967, remarried him in 1987.

The Chess Player

we come upon a conversation lull.
I hug my coffee cup
with my palms
as he tells me all about this guy—
smart as a book
he says—
who plays chess down at the park
from sunrise to dark.

"I go down there all the time.
I've never beaten him."

I say, "you're persistent."

he says, "we learn by losing."

with that he smiles—
proud of his thought,
I surmise.

I raise up my cup,
gesture it to him,
then I sip.

then another lull,
as dark thoughts slip
and patter about
in my head.

believe when I say

I do not wish to be
unkind,
or as the kids say:
induce a burn.
but truth is truth
and must be learned,
and so I press:

"if you've lost every time
to this same guy
over and over
turn after turn
and you've never won...
what I'd like to know,
I guess,
what exactly is it that
you learn?"

dealer wins

at the blackjack table
everyone has
a system

card counting
cutting thin
chip stacking
progressive betting
cutting thick
riding streaks

the dealer flicks the cards
one card up for each of us
and one card up
for the house
another card up for each of us
then one card hidden
upside down
for the house

thwip thwip thwip

the hands are dealt
aces and small cards
kings and queens
and jacks
"split it"
"hit that"
"double-down"
colorful cards all around

while one card sits
upside-down
resting hidden before
the dealer

everyone has a system
at the blackjack table
"I have a system"
they say
then go on and on
telling us all about it

they WIN a hand
"see it works," they say
then they lose
one or two
"that's to be expected"
and then a WIN
then they lose
lose
lose
WIN
lose
"it works over time"
lose
WIN
lose
lose
until they've lost
down to a point

where they stop promoting
their system

they
stop
talking
as
they are whittled down
down
down
to their last
chip

and they push it in

the dealer deals
2 kings

the player grins
the dealer winks
and shows a ten
then flips his hidden card
and it's an Ace

Blackjack!

the dealer wins
then takes the player's
final chip
who nods and stands

dabs his cigarette
in a tray of ash
pushes in his stool
whispers away
I presume
out of the casino
and into that much larger
harsher
game
where I hope he has a better
system
because
in that game
all the dealer's cards
are hidden

Carpology
(car·pol·o·gy)
n. (rare)

    *the serious or professional
study of seeds.*

hammered

wildflowers slouch lazy
in syrupy sunshine while
bumble bees swim
sleepily from one
open heart to another
stoned out of their minds
on ultraviolet alcohol
and narcotic nectar
while I lounge over here
in my chair
with a lean
getting high
off the scene

the first thing, if you really want to write

make sure your thermostat
gets adjusted right

too much heat
shortens thoughts
too much cold
and thoughts get dark

and humidity—no way!
it snuffs out every spark
and makes all thoughts
cliché
and everything made of paper
clings to your forearm
and dangles from your elbow

no
if you really want to write
it's gotta be a little cool
mostly dry like
late evenings after the rain
early mornings before
a hot summer day

and once the air
feels how you think
it should
then you just need—
and I can't stress this enough—
to fix the proper drink...

my wife's out of town
solitude's good for the soul
dishes multiply

here lies a fool

if you *don't* believe in God
graveyards make no sense—
the tombstone has no referent
you are no longer there
and will never be again

if you *do* believe in God
graveyards make no sense—
wherever you are it's not
in some vessel that rots
and will never be again

so whether you believe in God or not
graveyards make no sense—
but everyone believes in God
or they do not believe in God
yet tombstones cover the earth

a secret gift

man I felt good
today
July fourth
the year of our Lord
twenty-eighteen
what a blessing!
not because the holiday
(the bangs and pops
and spattering sparks
—I could care less
in fact prefer fire-
flies and frogs
and stars
in the dark)

but man I felt good
today
even though I worked
a sixteen hour shift
I still felt fast and light
quick of wit
but why?
I don't know
perhaps a gift

it felt so good
I hoped it would last
like a kind of seed
I didn't plant
but felt it grow

and expand
and lift and blossom from
a mighty root

as I
laughed and smiled
with manic moves
while nibbling from
its fruit

miracle at 3a.m.

the noise woke us both
it was 3 am
B was up in bed
I'd crashed on the couch
we met together
both groggy near
the kitchen

did you hear that?
yeah I heard it.
what was it?
I don't know.

we searched for damage
for shattered glass
or a broken branch
but found no such thing

we shrugged
we hugged
we returned to our beds
but it's hard to sleep
when you don't know the source
of a noise

I laid there recreating
the noise in my head
(another miracle we do
though we know not how)
I laid there replaying it

Bang! it was tinny
Bang! it was hollow
Bang! it was heavy

then I got it
threw off the covers
dashed to the bath
pulled the curtain back
looked down
there it was

a Family Size
shampoo bottle
freshly fallen
from some high ledge

once I knew what it was
and once I placed it back
I fell quick into sleep

all was well

although I never even thought
to wonder how
the bottle fell

hand written

you'd like my handwriting
folks compliment me on it
all the time and
I understand why
it reads easy
it pleases the eye

mom wouldn't tolerate poor
penmanship so I learned quick
to form each letter
clear and right
firm with grace
plump and light

I'm not one to gloat
but my words float
along upon the air
with perfect space
and little flair

"you can do better"
mom would declare

with every word I wrote
I felt her stare

but as for my grades
on my report
well
she didn't ever seem to care

the dealer won't wait forever

the dealer would shuffle
and I'd just sit there
playing with my chip stack,
or rubbing my fingertips
over the soft felt
atop the table while
other bozos tried
to talk to me.

that was the worst part
even during winning streaks—
    especially during winning streaks—
they'd want to talk.
they'd blow smoke,
dab their cigarettes,
sip their beer,
and have this look
like they just had to make noise
or they'd die.

we are each mysterious caverns,
pushing noises from our centers,
and everything we say
echoes through the filters
of our world views,
of our beliefs,
of our philosophies,
of our moral choices,
of our godliness.

well, these folks,
whom no doubt God loves,
they spoke and I don't
want to portray myself
better than them, but,
sitting there with them,
I'd think of Jesus
choosing his disciples
(real gamblers, eager
for light, hungry for God,
pushing in every chip
for a shot at something deep,
each disciple drunk with thoughts
of man and good and God),
while these dopes surrounding me
blew their smoke and struck
their pose with their chips
and their small dreams of financial gain,
whose words rang tinny,
and whose paths ran dull
and fruitless.

the shuffle ends.
the dealer grins.
the talking stops,
as the bozos place their bets
and watch the cards
flicked from the wrist,
and we gaze numb
through smokey light,

at the cards
we're dealt.

my first card's a three
of clubs
followed by a king
of hearts.

the dealer waits
for my call.

"hit me,"
I say,
then he flips over
another
card.

have you tried the special?

Friday comes late
old and gray
banging his fist
with a clatter
until I arrive
with the words
on the platter
which I scrape
medium rare
verse and line
on his plate.

I decided to go back to school

at work I'd read books
this particular job
had plenty of down time
the worst part though
coworkers would see the books I'd bring
and they would ask

"oh are you in school?"

I'd be sitting there
with some ten-pound book
open wide on my lap
as I scribbled thoughts and notes
along the margins
in the gaps
and they'd see the size
and nature
of the book and they'd ask

"oh are you in school?"

it could have been
a metaphysics book
a hermeneutics book
a social justice book
a cognitive psychology book
or the collected works
of some dead poet

I learned a sad fact

working those jobs
bringing those books to work:

reading difficult books
just for edification
well
that's not normal
and the people will require
an explanation

"oh are you in school" they'd ask

I'd say "no
just reading this
all on my own"

but that made things worse
because then they'd want
to talk about it

there I was reading
the dense articulation
of potent thinkers
men and women who
had devoted large portions
of their very lives
chasing insight on their topic
and some bozo would come along
and share their thought
which leapt haphazard
from the cognitive soup

of sitcom fragments and
internet memes
splashing around
in their happy heads

"what are you reading" they'd ask

I'd tell them something like
"philosophy of science"
and they'd offer something like
"I heard scientists are close
to making a time machine"
or "they say we only use ten percent
of our brain but that Einstein
used twice that much"

eventually I found it easier on my heart and
spirit
to tell them lies
I'd do just about anything
to avoid engaging
in such discussion

"are you in school" they'd ask

"yes I'm in school" I'd proclaim

"oh what are you studying" they'd ask

I'd shrug and say
"Spiritual Carpology"

no one gets away

listen to me church goers
listen to me home owners
listen to me all of you who have been
prequalified for a loan

  no one gets away
  with anything

travel bloggers building passive
income streams
public speakers selling people
worthless dreams
distraction addicts pushing content
to distracted masses
(from their Jesus tablets)
isolated rebels sitting neutered
on their asses
(tapping pixels on their power slabs)

  no one gets away
  with anything

self-righteous sign-readers
concealing all their cheats
dim-witted adventure seekers
achieving stupid feats
(just to prove their liberty)

listen to me born-agains
listen to me dead-to-sins

no one gets away
with anything

political cartoonists
enraging pessimistic minions
triggered parishioners
causing deep divisions
talentless actresses
nursing messianic complexes
(raising awareness for various sad realities)

no one gets away
with anything

it's nothing magic
like karma or
justice
it's simple cause
and effect
sub-atomic dominoes tilt
with every word
and fall
with every act

union workers
milking corporate clocks
prison guards
with hollow hearts
jocular judges
selling access to their gavels

no one gets away
with anything

listen to me greedy power brokers
listen to me undecided voters

it's simple cause
and effect
sub-atomic dominoes tilt
with every word
and fall
with every act

our God is a God
who grieves
yes even God loses things
he can't get back

now that's all I'm going to say
about all of that

if you're gonna learn to fly
you'd better learn to land

email management

so many emails
unread in a stack
emails emails emails
urgent alerts
important prompts
so many it hurts!
needing attention
needing response
too many to mention

reminders—
"I'll get to that soon"
directions—
"I'll need this for later"
requests—
"I don't have time right now"

so many emails
unread in a stack
and yet here I sit
refreshing the page
hoping you might
have emailed me back

everyone knows why Vincent van Gogh cut off his ear

he was a snake charmer
down on his luck
she was a moody
cobra

twitterpated romantics
sing about their passions
and all their satisfactions
galore

lovestruck bozos sing sing sing
while they dance dance
dance in through
ev'ry door

Vincent van Gogh alone at the bar
just doesn't want
to hear it
anymore

the lights have gone out

I look much like The Swamp Thing having
a coronary event when I swim—
if you could watch me in the water
you'd agree—
so you can see why
I go late to the pool,
when no one else is there
to witness the scene.

tonight something went wrong.
the lights were out.
it was dark.

I swam my laps, anyhow,
ten or so.

then after my swim,
while toweling off in the locker room,
some staff guy walks in
putting dirty towels
in his cart.

I say, "hey, the lights are out
in the pool. How do I turn them on?"

"they're on a timer," he says.

"well, they've been out three nights in a row."
"they're on a timer," he says again.
"I know, I get it, they're on a timer, but

the timer's wrong—they're shutting
off too early."

"not much we can do," he says, "it's all
hooked up to a timer."

I'm the persistent type, so I
employ reason and say, "okay,
but someone sets the timer, right?"

this seems to baffle him.

"who can I talk to about fixing the timer?"

he doesn't know.

I dry off, yank up my pants,
pull on my shirt,
slide on my sandals,
grab my bag and step
out into the August night.

I huff and look up
at the stars and the moon
and wonder what or whom
might save us from
our doom.

checkout is whenever

we were out on the deck
going back-and-forth
like we do
in the thick of some
conversation

when I
turned my head
looking toward the back
of our long deep yard
way way back

back to where
the grass is left uncut
and I saw his antlers there
emerging up
from the green
like a fallen branch

our conversation stopped
we both peered out
zoomed in as he
lifted up his mighty head
knowing he'd been seen
and then a doe lifted hers

they both laid there together listening
to the cicadas
to an ambitious woodpecker
to Lloyd three houses down

revving up his chainsaw
and then to an airplane
buzzing above our clouds

their ears flicked away bugs
as they stared at us
until they surmised
we posed no threat
meant no harm
then they relaxed again

and we were pleased
with ourselves
like Noah I suppose
on the day
his passengers came

we were pleased
to have a place
with shade from sun
a place that's safe
from cars and trucks
and hunter's guns

a place for wandering
beasts—majestic
guests—to come and lay
in tall cool grass
and get themselves
some needed rest

a close shave

from the waist up
I was naked
driving fast
a small battery powered razor
in my hand
pressed firm
to my cheek
vibrating and grinding
tough stubble

I was real excited
about a new job
at this Italian cafe
I couldn't be late
but the problem was
I overslept
and had to shave
and get all dressed
in the car
on the way

traffic was light
my hair was a mess
my shirt on the seat
to my right

then my shaver battery
grew weak
(and this is the crisis of the tale)
but I kept pushing it

all over my face
(what else could I do?)
as the gears
I could hear
ground slower
and slower

and

sl o w   e   r

and pulled on my hairs
until finally it died
in the heart of its grind
on the dense heavy stubble
of my chin

the blades wouldn't move
froze-up in mid chew
and clamped to the hairs
an inch or two
beneath my low lip

it hurt when I pulled
and I couldn't let go
without terrible pain
so my hand was stuck
up on my face too

I stopped at a store

with this machine on my face
and stood in a line
and the patrons all stared
but I looked straight ahead
like it was nothing and life
was just fine
but the manager saw me
and pointed to a sign
on the door

I had neither shirt
nor shoes on my feet
but I showed her my chin
and implored her
to help
and she did

and everyone watched
my battery act
as I did the whole thing
all with one hand—
paid for the pack
opened them up
ejected the dead
inserted the fresh
then went out the door
to finish my shave
and free the machine
from off of my face

I burst into to work
tucking my shirt
assembling my tie
with just enough time
to swallow a breadstick
or two
in life there's a line
it's firm yet it's fine
between keeping your life
whole and secure
and in your control
or being taken apart
by chaos and chance
and each of us learn
to walk that fine line
and some of us
occasionally
dance.

old dirt

I'm sitting easy in
my lawn chair out front
oatmeal bowl
steaming in
the early air

a dump truck soon
will come and dump
a mound of dirt
for our new patio
and I wait here
for delivery.

I scoop a spoon
of steaming mush
up from my breakfast
bowl to my awaiting
mouth (the days of eggs
and bacon long long gone)

a motorcycle putters by
the driver smiles
careful with his safety
helmet and his protective
mustache as
the sun ascends slow
in the sky to make
her daily payment and
a Monarch butterfly
freshly hatched

dries his showroom wings
preparing for
his big long flight to
the deep deep south.

I take another bite
of old man mush knowing
I am going to break
a sweat today

digging up old earth then
replacing it with something
new.

I just know I'm going
to sweat today and I take
a bigger swig of bottled
water as my neighbor's dog
terrifies an industrious squirrel
who hustles up
a Maple tree
and I look down the street
and wait

and wait

and wait

for my

delivery.

my meeting got bumped so I'm walking around Grand Avenue for a while

it's that part of town
everyone likes
with hotshot bars
and fancy cafes
and the stores with the names
no one can pronounce
with brick and glass
framing the fronts
(overflowing dumpsters
hidden in back)

people going in and coming out

there's a girl on a date
she laughs
much too hard at his joke

there's a mom on a phone
she acts real mad
at her tantruming boy

there's a dude in a suit
who pretends
he's not broke

up and down the street
the sun shines reflects
off the congestion
of cars

which ignites the old street
like a river of jewels
deep
in a puddle of light

and I walk around
in this counterfeit realm
where everything's housed
in a decorative shell

yes I walk around
where nothing is what
it pretends to be
where ev'rything's
layered in fake

even the sky
is not really blue
the pastries and rolls
come delivered pre-cooked
then are placed on display
in the bakery case
(and a muffin's just a small
piece of cake)
those ropes don't really hold
that bridge in the air
and those lifeboats in the bar are there
just for looks
and the clouds
they're just mountains

that float

and I walk around
in this counterfeit realm
peeling the shells
removing the masks
fixing my gaze
clenching my teeth
trying to give air
to whatever it is
that suffers
beneath

the roller coaster goes slow at the top

we stayed at an upstart resort
with two pools
in Fort Myers Beach
across the street
from the Royal Scoop
and the Tuckaway
Cafe

the heat was great
and it rained a short rain
every day
just after lunch

I liked this time
in our lives
a held-breath rest
at the top
of the roller coaster track
the future
about to come fast
with possible thrill
or possible crash
you with your profitable work
me with my upcoming book

both of us aware
of our own limitations
you with your clashes with stress
me with my financial mess

both of us seeking
the truth about God
you with your suspicions of Christ
and me with my stained-glass eyes

I liked this time
in our lives
with you in a sundress
me in my shorts
watching the sun go down
in slow-motion
as we strolled
hand-in-hand
past the port
on the shore
of the ocean

mangoes

mangoes drop from trees
with a thud
down here
and we
are thrilled by this

mangoes for us
back home
they're like nine dollars each
and so
it's a pretty cool thing
to pick them free
up off the grass

all that falls from trees
back home
are pine cones
crab apples
dead sticks
Peeping Toms
and Cottonwood seeds

the folks down here
though
don't think much of it
apparently—
they step right over each

familiarity fosters

depreciation
I guess

but it's new for us
and I
bend down
gather one up
from off the ground
hold it up to Barbara
like a mighty gem
and our eyes go wide
and we grin

peace goes to the loser of the race

I was in a foul mood
and getting real sick of stoplights
  hurry up and go
  hurry up and stop
another rat in the congested hustle
eager drivers jamming up my rear
squeezing me from ev'ry side
pulling sudden in my lane
dangerously close to my hood
like manic runaway brides
causing static in my brain
until I threw up my arms
and slowed myself down
to a slothful obstinate pace

and that's when things got good
the rats rushed madly away
my truck was now in empty space
and like some magic divination
all the lights stayed green
and I moved like Moses
straight on through
to my destination

learning about rock

the music was hard and dopey,
just some burned out bozo
standing on the stage
yelling over-and-over:

"I WANT TO ROCK!"

What does that even mean?

apparently
it means
little more than yelling
over and
over, and
over:

"I WANT TO ROCK!"

into a microphone,
like an imbecile,

in a big room crowded
with other burned out bozos
gazing up and wanting
to do exactly
the same.

"If you're faced with a forced landing, fly the thing as far into the crash as possible."

Bob Hoover, *revolutionized modern aerobatic flying, worked at a grocery store to pay for pilot training, and once successfully poured himself a cup of tea while performing a barrel roll.*

five bucks

I've got this five dollar bill
it's from 1950
had it for a year or so now
probably not worth much more
than five bucks

but

I'm having a hard time letting it go
it's the inverted value
that's what holds me to it
that's what gets me
the 68 year
transformation

in 1950 I could've filled
my truck with gas
and still had cash
left over to buy
an egg sandwich
and a Coke

and now as I hold this bill
between my thumb
and fingers
part of me must think
that old value
somehow
still lingers
within it

history is narrative

it's a long drive
to Mukwonago
from Maplewood

B and I pass the time
discussing the divinity
of Christ

Mark's gospel
in all of it's face-slapping concision
proclaims Christ as God
not directly like
the other gospels but
right there in the structure
of the narrative itself

what bothers B is that
to her
playing with the narrative
sabotages the historicity

I lift my hand off the wheel
to gesture
"why can't a historical event
be true while the narrative
about that same event
also be true?"

she looks forward
thinking and

gnawing on a flaw
she senses
deep down
somewhere in the layers

she fails to find it on the drive
she can't yet quite get at it

when she finds it
brushes it off
exposes it to light
her faith will swell
or perhaps her faith
will fall apart

in the meantime
the road goes on
another mile
the sky stays blue
and I smile
a multi-dimensional smile
grateful to be near her mind

as our little car
putters through
Baraboo

in search of permanent liberation

now
tail lights as far as I can see
morning rush hour
limp drizzle
skies gray

I'm running late

now
I decide to exit on Broadway
maybe cut through Northeast
it's a longshot but
then again
all my plans are longshots

the side streets look good
until one bozo
after another
emerges out of some dark nowhere
to block me off and we all
slow to a crawl

now
I'm weaving around
and in-and-out
trucks and cars
and city busses

now
the traffic breaks

I press the gas
accelerate into open space
my ego radiates
in new found liberty and
my face smacks peach with glee
as I even think I hear
my guardian angel sing

until the next cluster
of anxious tail lights
appear before me

now
I tap the brakes
and assume my place
back in the sad
flow of things

smooth jazz for martyrs

they lit Justin Martyr on fire
tied him to a post
and when the flames
took to his flesh
he looked the crowd in the eyes
and laughed

they crucified Peter upside-down
lowered him into a hole
buried him just like that
in the dark with blood rushing
to his head as earth squeezed him
from every side and he closed
his eyes and he smiled

they pierced Thomas with four spears
thrusted by four soldiers
and the punctures were lethal
and Thomas knew it
as he lifted his dying arms and
ran his shimmering fingers
into his own mortal wounds
for proof

Simon, Jude, Philip, and Andrew
were crucified

Bartholomew and James
were beaten dead

Matthew and James (the son
of Zebadee)
were run through with
a blade

I've never been much for pain
(it hurts)
I don't even like spicy food

yet I seek the Lord
like a treasure and try
to conform my heart to Christ and his
magnetic insanity

so when the powers that be
come around for their measure
and their violent pleasure
I can't help but wonder

what are they going to do
to me?

a great light has dawned

the wicked in the penthouse
the righteous in a rut

but God is looking down
for people looking up

impromptu engineers

life is like trying to build
an airplane
while falling from some great height
in the sky
you gather what pieces you find
falling around you
in front and behind
you attach and adhere
this on to that
still falling fast
checking your time

until

you try your thing out
switching its gears
pulling its cranks
turning its wheels
bouncing off trees
bursting through leaves
snapping through branch

until

something works!
you're leveling out!
you even move upward!
the trees are now where they should be
beneath your feet
and look how far you can see!

and the trembling and shaking all cease
and you take it all in
and even find joy in the ride
and life even strikes you as grand
adventurous
meaningful
planned

until

you run out of gas
and must now figure out
what it means
to land

...LURING A CROWD TO SEE
WHATEVER MESSAGE
YOUR AUDACIOUS HEART
WANTS THEM
TO SEE...

building a rose

everyone knows
you can't yank a stem
to bring forth a rose

when working with flowers
you leave them alone
untouched in dull soil
to fritter the days
to daydream the hours
under day's holy glow
under night's holy show

when working with flowers
just leave them alone
only then will they grow

the accusation

I'm driving my truck looking
for a free parking spot
(only suckers pay to park),
over by the hospital,
Riverside Avenue.

that's where this two-door car
(the color of marshmallow
tainted slightly by a flame)
kept driving up my ass,
tottering and swerving,
like he wanted to pass.

well I wasn't afflicted and I
just hate to be a burden,
so no big deal to me, I
pulled off to the side
to let him drive by.

but he wanted to talk,
so we rolled down our windows
and I said, "hi."

but this guy was swollen
with wrath and spat forth
dramatic attack, with shifty eyes
and one long infuriated finger
held hard at little ol' me.

"you fuck you," he said,

and, "you got your gun?
you want to go shoot me?"

"no, no," I said,
and I meant it.

"don't you give me magic eyes."

"what?"

"you cast your fuck spell
on me with black-magic eyes?"

"I don't think I am who
you think I am."

his finger hovered toward me
and his face still held rigid,
so I got all friendly on him.
"no, see, *blessings*. I cast
blessings on you—many
many many blessings."

he softened his face,
put his finger back
in its holster, and said,
"okay okay, blessings
to you—many."

then he drove away

and I never saw him again, and
I turned my radio up where
a cheerful voice shared a good
report about the weather, and
a crow swooped down to nab
a crust of bread over by
the picnic tables, at just the moment when
an old van vacated a parking spot
several feet in front of me.

so I parked my truck.
got out.
took a good breath
of early morning air
and grinned at my
abundant
luck.

**sometimes imagination is the only
thing that keeps my heart**

I see people here and there
(nowadays I see them
everywhere)
you've seen them too
people pressed under the sweaty thumb
of have-it-all hustlers
and wannabe tycoons

people who displease
the haughty eyes
of each and every
self-embalmed passer-by
that drive along
in massive cars
all alone
while talking loud
on mobile phones

I see them these
competition victims
loitering about
outside the stores
in neglected alleys
hanging around forgotten
dumpsters

I see them
they are real

people
who think nothing about Paleo
who know little about Tinder
who are, however, quite familiar
with minimalism
(but not the type you're thinking of)

I see these people
and the accumulation of their days
manifested on their clothes
and in their hair
I see the accumulation
of nutritionless meals
on their faces
in their strides
I see their fading proportions
and their three-dimensional
deteriorations

I see them fall apart
within my reach but behind
perplexing barriers
too thick
too high
to overcome

but my heart beats toward them
and I imagine these folks
at my table scooping their favorite foods
on some Thanksgiving Day

and I see them go back
to the buffet
and they
can't even hide their smirk
as they smile off old habits
of guilt and conservation
as they lift the heaping scoop
above their waiting plate

the ghost of Abraham Lincoln's sock

the lunch bag dangled
from my hand
as I walked through town
passing all the people,
none of them aware
of the horrors
inside.

the bag contained a mouse,
whose head was snapped
in the jaws
of a vicious trap.

I suppose I could have disposed of the sack
at home, but
didn't want the smell
of death.

so I was roaming around looking
for a place to dispose it.

I roamed around among
the men and women
with their friends,
with their coats,
with their phones,
with their kids,
with their canes.
they passed by,

and I watched them,
like I do, and,
as I searched for a proper trash,
and with death on my mind,
I thought about ghosts.

people claim to have seen them.
sometimes they see them
with vivid clarity.
they don't even know,
sometimes at first,
the person they're seeing is dead.

so that's what I was thinking about
as I walked around with my mouse
in a bag.

in particular, what interested me
was that I'd never heard a person claim
to see a naked ghost.

no, they're always clothed.

but, see, that means the shirt of a ghost,
or their Victorian dress,
or their blue-collar boots,
or whatever else they wear,
all those clothes must be
phantasmic, too.

and I wondered what would happen

if a ghost took off his shirt
and left it there, say,
on a porch swing.

would that apparition of apparel dangle there,
glowing with a dim, haunted light?

or, do our clothes bind with us, somehow,
in death?

well, I didn't have an answer and
both ideas struck me as silly.

but I found a little trash receptacle
just outside a hardware store.

I jammed the bag into the push-door
and walked on.

I happened to see my reflection
in the window of the store.

a reflection, in a way,
exists much like a ghost,
and I took note
of mine, and,
in particular,
everything
he wore.

I took a number. There's no place to sit.

it's not that life itself
is boring
things do happen
exciting things
things we'll tell
our neighbors
our friends
our family
and people we want to impress
at parties

we'll go into passionate
detail
all about
funny accidents
drunken fights
near death experiences
wardrobe malfunctions
run-ins with the law

things happen all the time

but most of life
we fritter away
waiting around
trying to conjure up
the next thing

took a long shower
decided to go to church
the internet's out

counting to one hundred

on the day I learned to count
up to one hundred
mom
picked me up
from school.

she turned the radio down
and asked,
"what did you learn today?"

at just that moment
sunshine shot
like a spotlight
from behind an old cloud,
all the way down from the Lord,
through my open window,
right on top of me.

then I—without pomp
or ostentation,
or lengthy
introduction—
began counting:

one.
two.
three.

all the way up
through the teens.

I watched her marvel
as I counted on,
up through the twenties.

but her expression changed
at about thirty-three,
like some dull ghost
possessed her.

thirty-eight.
thirty-nine.

a stoplight flicked red
and she brought the car
to a stop,
just as I approached
forty-two.

at forty-three, she
flung up her waving hands
and pled:

"okay, okay, please stop,
that's good, Danny,
that's fine."

I fell silent.
the light turned green
and our car puttered
forward.

mom turned up the radio tunes
as I stared out the window,
enduring the lonely pangs
of genius.

focus on the family

one of the roles
of family
I suppose
must be to insulate the child
from dark topics
like death
and mortality

these kids
—I see it all the time—
they get sucked into a flow
of life
of daily tasks
and daily class
of school
and camps
and then degrees
from universities
and onward to careers
and retirement dreams
they get so frothed up
in the carnival of living
they fail to ask
about life itself

but not kids like me
we grew up
with our ears unplugged
with no bumper cushions in the gutter

and man
I tell you
our brains
get triggered young
by the strange
double-sided
puzzle

that we should be here at all
in this playground called life
that we should even breathe
and exist
without consent
and then
we're told
we will be taken
away again

remember that feeling?
when death was strange?
when it made no sense?

there it was
the unveiled tyrant

but then the coin
it turns again
we've seen so many things
eventually decay
and all the things that go away

and every thing we love that dies

the passing days they tip us
past a crucial line
past a turning point
where it's the thought of endless life
that smacks as strange

yes and then
we endure the change
where somehow
immortality
(not mortality)
quite suddenly
seems the true
absurdity

SUPER NOVA

our back yard,
it's impressive
—over an acre!
tall trees,
tall grasses,
rabbits and squirrels,
and endless things
that chirp.

we're dog-sitting
all weekend long
(energetic puppy
already 50 pounds).

she jumps around
on the couch,
off the couch,
over the couch.

her name's Nova.

she's untrained.
pulls the leash.
races through spaces,
out to the porch,
into my office,
back to the kitchen
—where she stops
(slides on the rug).

she sees our back yard
through the patio door.
her eyes swell,
her tail goes nuts,

all that space!
all that nature!

she scratches the glass with a paw.
how does one get there?
perhaps there's a door
down on the floor,
so back-and-forth she goes,
nose to the boards.

there has to be a way!

along the wall,
along the patio door
—all that nature
to explore,
if there's no door
what a waste!

she tries the window
on the stairs
—no chance.

she tries the window
in the bathroom

— too high.

she dashes back-n-forth,
round-and-round until
she muffs and sighs,
sits at the glass
(almost cries),
resigns herself
to dreaming.

later that night
I go for my run.
Lake Harriet.
just before midnight
when the stars are so bright—
practically loud.

I stop to stare
at the expanse
—all that space!
each bright star
a fantastic place
to explore.

I have this sense
(I can't explain)
that somehow
someday
I'll visit each.
I know I will
though I know not how

(what a waste
if we won't).

There has to be a way!

for now I resign
myself to dreaming,
still trapped
behind the glass
of planet earth.

I shrug,
begin my long run,
round-and-round
Lake Harriet,
pulling hard
on my leash.

happy here

silly little me
at night
happy here
alone
dog asleep in her crate
wife asleep upstairs in her bed
like a bird in her nest

happy here
pen in hand dancing
around some sad
epiphany

happy here
at my little desk
in our little house
engulfed by the anxious song
of little crickets

happy here
mocking death
which lurks so near
I can almost touch it
and when I reach for it
everything else shifts
further away

happy here
with my poems and my books
my old drawings

and that old neglected reading
chair

happy here
in the mellow calm
breathing easy
wearing nothing more
than boxers and
this black one-pocket shirt

happy here
knowing full well
that anything can happen
at any time
on any day
and
it's probably going
to hurt

YOU'D BETTER HAVE

SOMETHING TO SAY...

...WORTH LOOKING UP FOR.

nudging the sprouts

we've got this lousy patch
of unkempt lawn along the west
side of our drive

B planted wildflowers there
along with several giant
sunflowers

we go out every day
to check for growth but it's mostly
still unwanted weeds

dandelion and crab grass
and other nutrient robbing pests
unworthy of names

we're out there today
bent over zooming in on what
might be blooming

with her finger she nudges
a sprout the size of a paperclip
"I think this is one"

I nudge one too though don't
really know what nudging will do
"what about this one?"

she comes over and touches it
"I think that's just a weed but
it might be a flower"

frogs are singing down at the pond
a passing car flicks headlights on
a neighbor closes his garage

I jump to my feet and look
over at B standing by the St Francis statue
and she says with alarm "what is it?"

I look to the north and then to the east
twirl around as I look to the sky and reply
"I thought I felt a nudge"

Dan Kent has thrilled thousands with his poetry and writing. His style has been called thoroughly approachable, suprising, refreshing, sincere, and hilarious. One astute critic summarized Dan's poetry as "Socrates meets Jack Handey."

You can follow Dan at:

twitter.com/thatdankent

facebook.com/authorDanielKent

Other books by Dan Kent:

The Training of KX12
Volume One

The Training of KX12
Volume Two

Diamonds Mixed with
Broken Glass

Confident Humility
Becoming Your Full Self without
Becoming Full of Yourself

Made in the USA
Lexington, KY
06 December 2019